Recommendations

"When someone is grieving—experiencing the loss of a love⟨d one⟩ ⟨...⟩ direct their thoughts, actions, and feelings. We all process l⟨oss in very personal⟩ ways and that timeline can look so different to each of us. I have witnessed this process of grief in Jacke Van Woerkom. She acknowledges the real aspect of pain and grief, yet doesn't allow it to take anything else away from her family. Jacke has distilled her journey, offering all her love, grace and dignity, to those going through that same process, and made it into something authentically tangible in Grieving Moms, Finding Hope. The foundational activities and action steps found in the Grieving Moms Participant Guide, equip those dealing with such pain, creating in them the mindset they need to get through this challenging time. I fully endorse this program and Jacke's work, for she has the skills and heart to help others navigate the grieving process."

Kathrine Lee
Life Coach & Business Strategist Author
Founder of The Pure Hope Foundation
Frequent Guest, Oprah Winfrey Show

"This one-of-a-kind program helps Grieving Moms by giving them the support and encouragement they need to face a devastating loss—the death of their child! Jacke gives us a great visual when she calls it a Landslide. **Grieving Moms, Finding Hope** offers a process to help these precious women dig their way out from under the rubble together, in a community that provides a safe place to feel, cry and heal. Due to my own pain over the choices and lifestyle of my daughter, and after years of working with women who have felt pain and heartache because of the choices of their adult children, I began the support community of *Hurting Moms, Mending Hearts*. Just like I did, Jacke has taken her pain and extended her hand to others who feel lost in despair. I highly recommend **Grieving Moms, Finding Hope** to moms who now find themselves in a club that none of them wanted to join. In this community, they will discover that hope and healing are possible through the power of God's love. If you are a Grieving Mom this is your new beginning."

Cathy Taylor
Founder, *Hurting Moms, Mending Hearts*

Who better to write **Grieving Moms, Finding Hope** than Jacke, who has walked and continues to walk this "Landslide" while allowing God to use her to help others along the way. I believe God is going to use this study to bring moms closer to Him and to comfort them as they go through the most difficult season of their life.

Liz Puffer
Care Minister, Saddleback Church

Recommendations

"Purposeful, passionate and persevering…I watched Jacke Van Woerkom walk through this 'Landslide' of loss with courage and grace. For all of us who have endured the loss of someone near and dear to us, the valleys are deep and the terrain difficult, but we must journey on. God did not suggest we camp in the "the valley of the shadow of death," but it is one we must pass through. Jacke has done this, holding fast to the hope of Him, the Victor, one step, one breath at a time. **Grieving Moms, Finding Hope** is a result of that process."

Judy Blue
Author of *Money Matters for Parents and Their Kids, Your Kids Can Master Their Money, Raising Money-Smart Kids, Money Talks and So Can We*

"Grief is a reality. Sorrow is non-negotiable. Pain is inevitable. Jacke Van Woerkom has not only experienced the anguish life brings, she has confronted life's agitating moments with authenticity, candor and resolve. Not being a subscriber to a quick fix or a microwave approach to heartache, Jacke provides biblical and practical advice to not only survive through hurt, but provides a healthy process to thrive during the suffering. I greatly respect and appreciate Jacke's heart for those struggling and I'm confident this book will provide healing for many souls."

Randy Ponder
Lead Pastor, Morro Bay Police Chaplain
SLO County Sheriff Chaplain

Every person at some time in their life encounters a Landslide of their own. The concepts and encouragement shared by Jacke's tragic experience can help any hurting heart. Instead of shutting down and closing in, Jacke unselfishly allowed others to journey through her healing process. Her life of bravery and boldness serves as an inspiration of amazing possibilities by surrendering to God's power and grace.

Anita Sirianni
ANSIR International

Grieving Moms
FINDING HOPE
Resurfacing

Copyright © 2017 by Jacke Van Woerkom and Sherry Lynn Ward

SQUARE TREE PUBLISHING
www.SquareTreePublishing.com

All Rights Reserved.
This book is protected by the copyright laws of the United States of America. No part of this publication may be reproduced, stored in a retrieval system, or transmitted, in any form or by any means- electronic, mechanical, photocopying, recording, or otherwise – without prior written permission from the author. For more information please contact info@SquareTreePublishing.com

▸ For More Information

SQUARE TREE PUBLISHING
info@SquareTreePublishing.com
www.SquareTreePublishing.com

To contact the author or for bulk book orders:
www.SquareTreePublishing.com

▸ Scripture References

All Scripture quotations, unless otherwise indicated, are taken from the Holy Bible, New International Version®, NIV®. Copyright ©1973, 1978, 1984, 2011 by Biblica, Inc.™ Used by permission of Zondervan. All rights reserved worldwide. www.zondervan.co m The "NIV" and "New International Version" are trademarks registered in the United States Patent and Trademark Office by Biblica, Inc.™

▸ Cover and Interior Design

Cathy Nelson Arkle - The Thumbprint Group

ISBN: 978-1-7329587-2-2

Welcome Letter From Jacke

On January 15th, my son Randall Lawrence Van Woerkom completely lost hope because of what life handed him and by his wrongful choice on how to resolve it. He attempted to send his family to Heaven so they wouldn't have to suffer from the shame he had caused them. I believe God sent His angels into that place of desperation and said, "No! No, you will not be the one who has a say so in your family taking their last breath." Miraculously, my daughter-in-love, her father and my two little warrior grandsons survived his attempt.

The countless amount of incoming and outgoing phone calls that occurred throughout that evening and into the early morning hours could only be described as being buried and frozen deep beneath a landslide.

Two days before my son's passing, I went to Yosemite all alone to do what I like to call, "Kneeling and Healing" after the Christmas chaos in our house. I'm by nature, an introvert, requiring alone time to get filled back up. I went out to snow shoe on a trail off the beaten path. I looked to my right and as Stevie Nicks quoted in her song *Landslide*, "I saw my reflection in the snow-covered hills...'Til the landslide brought it down."

A couple weeks after my landslide hit, I was watching one of *The Lord of the Rings* movies with my other son Ryan. We watched the scene where the hobbits were crossing over the snowy mountain when they too, were buried beneath a sudden landslide. One by one they resurfaced, gasping for air and mentally wrestling with irrational thoughts for their survival. The camera then zooms into the aged face of Gandolph. The lines on his face etched by experiential wisdom. My son looked at me, no words were exchanged, but at that moment, our hearts united in agreement of feeling the same as they did. I immediately related to Gandolph and that I was chosen to lead this family up and out of our landslide. I needed to summit this mountain, seek hope, breathe in this thin air, and view from above how God wanted us to proceed.

The verse that God kept bringing to my mind is 2 Corinthians 4:8-10 where it says, *"We are hard pressed on every side, but not crushed; perplexed, but not in despair; persecuted, but not abandoned; struck down, but not destroyed. We always carry around in our body the death of Jesus, so that the life of Jesus may also be revealed in our body."*

Your experience may also feel like you were buried by a sudden landslide. When it happened, your body, mind and spirit froze just long enough to be protected. The only manual that brings hope is God's Word and in it His promises.

Welcome Letter From Jacke cont.

Through this Grieving Moms support group, we are reaching out to grab your hand in hopes that you'll take it and journey with us to find hope and healing in your journey. You are not alone! We bring no scales to the group. No one's pain is greater than another's. Pain is pain. We are here to help you every step of the way to come out of your personal landslide.

We will journey on this trail experiencing all the phases and emotions together. We will delicately nudge you to keep going because, *"Being confident of this, He who began a good work in you will complete it until the day of Christ Jesus."* Phil. 1:6

Some days you will feel like putting on your boots and marching toward your peak and other days you'll want to be in your slippers and simply hear Him speak. No matter where you are in your progress, we pray you will find the hope and healing you deserve!

Though the mountains be shaken and the hills be removed, yet my unfailing love for you will not be shaken nor my covenant of peace be removed, says the Lord, who has compassion on you.
Isaiah 54:10 NIV

(Written from a remote part of the big island of Hawaii secluded in a treehouse.)
My prayer: "Dear Father, give me the words from Heaven, into my heart, into my head and through my hands. What do I do with the loss of my beautiful son, Randall Van Woerkom?"
"Give them Hope, Jacke."

DEDICATION

We would like to dedicate this book to

all the Grieving Moms,

who have lost their way and

need the hope to resurface

after their Landslide.

Jacke and Sherry

Acknowledgements

We would like to thank and acknowledge the following people for making this curriculum possible:

Sherry Lynn Ward

- **My husband,** Rolf, who without his love and support this book would not be possible. Thank you to my children, Megan, Caleb, and Bryce who are the inspiration for what I do.

- **Jacke Van Woerkom** thank you for your tremendous courage and tenacity to climb up and out of your own personal Landslide, while selflessly helping other Grieving Moms. It is a testament to the true love that Jesus shows.

- **Cathy Taylor** for her belief and leadership in this program and for her support and dedication to all the Hurting Moms and Grieving Moms.

- **Square Tree Team**

    Melodie Fox for her amazing content editing and helping me to become a better writer.

    Monica Bosque for her constant attention to detail for the final edits.

    Cathy Arkle for her absolutely stunning design of the graphics to give the Grieving Moms something beautiful to have and to look at.

Acknowledgements

Jacke Van Woerkom

- **My Courageous Family**, the survivors of my horrific Landslide: Marcai, Jim, Noah, Jack, Larry my supportive husband of 35 years, my sons, Randy, Ryan & Mitchell Van Woerkom, Krysten & Greyson, Chelsea, my Daddy…Joe, my beautiful mom Franke who is in Heaven with Randy, Christine, my sister Nikke, my brother Eddie, my sister-in-law Anne and their kids: Nicholas, Dane & Delaney.

- **Team Cheyenne:** Matt & Kristin, Kristin's mom Sue, Paul & Kristin, Stacie, Annalisa, Brandon & Lindz and the beautiful staff at Cheyenne Regional Medical Center, Cheyenne Paramedics and all the other angels that showed up in our very frozen state.

- **Saddleback Church Family** — Anna, Cynthia, Jane, Colleen and David, Liz Puffer, Janice the angel that brings a smile to all that walk through the Ministry Center doors, Pastor Rick & Kay Warren who have been undeniably the two most genuine models of Christ to me and my family since 1997 and now we share this hopeful, yet devastating journey of losing our sons to suicide. Pastor Tom & Chaundel also beautiful models of Christ and supportive friends through our Landslide. Amanda of Trinity Counseling, Counselors: Colleen & Connie. Sean & Lishele, Lindsey S., Rachel, & Lindsey K., Brian and Brad, Anthony & Michelle, Greg & Kat, Michelle & Jayme. My Meadowood Family, Ralph & Barb M., Randy and Mary D., and to those of you that gave of your time and finances that gifted us anonymously and all of you I may have not mentioned due to the overwhelming and loving response when we were frozen.

- **Special thanks to my Earth Angel:** Cathy Chambers who is the most selfless person I know and her husband Dave for sharing Cathy during the darkest part of our Landslide.

- **The Trail Angels.**

- **Melissa Jensen**, I wouldn't have the hope to continue breathing without your perseverance and bravery for leading me to Jesus Christ back in 1996. Where would we be without the hope of Heaven and to see our children after we complete our mission here on earth? He is a good God!

- **My Soul Sisters:** Carmen, Julie, Katie & Kathrine.

- **Judy Blue** and **Sandy Leonard** who have been strong spiritual mentors in my life and true prayer warriors.

- **Grieving Moms Finding Hope Family:** Millie, Didi, Jani, Lisa, Isobel, Barb, Carrie and Michele.

- **Sherry Ward** thank you for believing in me and your relentless grace in co-writing this with me as I climbed up and out of the Landslide. You've been an answer to prayer which was to one day write a book to inspire women and give them hope. Your love and hard work invested in me and this beautiful project WILL be a true blessing to all of us courageous moms for many years to come. To God be the glory!

Purpose of Grieving Moms, Finding Hope

🗝 Each **Grieving Moms, Finding Hope (GMFH)** support group provides an opportunity for Grieving Moms to come alongside one another as they bear the pain, learn to work through their grief, and offer tools to help move forward through the grieving process.

> Sharing our stories, our hurt, and our pain with one another is a major part of this group. Some of the moms have never talked about their Landslide to anyone outside of the family. By talking about it in a safe place, the pain begins to diminish, and by listening to each other they begin to understand that they are not alone. The most significant part of the healing happens because of these two elements of the group – talking and listening.

🗝 Each **GMFH** support group hopes to encourage members to grow in their relationship with Jesus as we learn to trust Him through the grieving process.

> You will be using a lot of Scripture as you go through this program. Some of the women in your group may be totally unfamiliar with the Bible or with the healing power of Jesus. In addition to learning how to trust Him in the midst of their Landslide, our prayer is that they will begin to realize that He is the answer to having joy and peace again in every area of their lives.

🗝 The ultimate goal is for each **Grieving Mom** to resurface after the Landslide has hit and to find the hope and friendship to move forward through the pain.

> There is a tremendous amount of freedom when we begin to recognize that God is in control even after the Landslide. At first, we may have to give God our grief every few hours or even every few minutes. Eventually though, we begin to realize that God is always faithful in giving us "the peace that surpasses all understanding". All we have to do is ask.

Welcome Grieving Moms, Finding Hope Leaders

I want to thank you for stepping up to lead a *Grieving Moms, Finding Hope* group. I believe that your desire to lead this group is actually a calling from God. He has intentionally chosen you for this important role for which He will equip you with everything you need to lead effectively.

Grieving Moms, Finding Hope is designed to provide a safe place where women can share their pain with other moms who are experiencing the grief of losing a child, which we call a Landslide. By the end of the twelve (12) weeks they will have received a tremendous amount of healing, and they will have grown closer to each other and to the God who loves them beyond anything they can imagine.

As the leader of this group, you have the privilege of guiding these women through the material. Within a few weeks, you will begin to see the group bond and begin to share their deepest pain. They will also learn how to receive the perfect peace that only He can give in the midst of their grief.

Don't forget that your most important function as the leader of this group is to maintain the guidelines which will ensure that it is a safe place for sharing. Your job is not to "fix" the other women, or even to offer them advice, but to encourage and support them by keeping them on track as they move through the study from week to week.

God always shows up in these groups! He will use everyone's sharing to touch someone else in the group, and He will be the one to help the women to heal through this process. Be careful not to get in the way of what He wants to do.

May God richly bless you and may you experience his incredible grace as you allow Him to use you to lead the women in your group toward healing and freedom from the pain of being a *Grieving Mom*.

Jacke Van Woerkom & Sherry Lynn Ward

Leading a Grieving Moms, Finding Hope Group

WHO SHOULD LEAD A GMFH GROUP?
1. Leaders should be women who have experienced the pain of being a Grieving Mom themselves.
2. Leaders should have a relationship with Jesus Christ and demonstrate spiritual maturity.
3. Leaders should be able to offer hope to the women in the group through their own sharing.
4. Leaders should have a sense of calling to lead a GM group.

HOW ARE GM LEADERS EQUIPPED?
1. Leaders should be accountable to a member of the church staff.
2. Experienced leaders should be mentoring potential or new leaders.
3. Leaders should be equipped with a GM Leader Guide and a Bible.

WHERE SHOULD YOU START?
1. View your GM Leader Guide and familiarize yourself with the material.
2. Register your church or group by emailing us at info@GrievingMoms.com
3. Check out the additional resources at www.GrievingMoms.com

WHAT DETAILS SHOULD YOU BE THINKING ABOUT?

1. *Where will you meet?*
   Most groups meet at a church or in someone's home. Because of the delicate and confidential nature of the topic, it is not advised to meet in a public place, such as a coffee shop or restaurant.

2. *What day and time of the week will you meet?*
   You will want to check your church calendar before choosing the day of the week and time you will meet. If you run more than one group per year, you may want to consider having them on different nights to accommodate more women.

3. *How will you publicize the group?*
   Before starting a group, it is important to let people know about it. Some suggestions for getting the word out are the church bulletin, a website, social media, flyers, an information table, etc.

4. *Will you have childcare?*
   You will need to determine ahead of time whether you will offer it or not at the church.

Leading a Grieving Moms, Finding Hope Group

5. ***Will you have refreshments?***
   Refreshments are optional.

6. ***Provide Name Tags.***
   Name tags are a great idea, especially for the first few weeks until you get to know each other.

7. ***Have tissue available at meetings.***
   There will definitely be tears shed in your group. Having a box of tissue in the middle of the room where everyone can get to it is advisable.

HOW LONG DOES A HMMH SUPPORT GROUP LAST?

1. The GM support group consists of twelve (12) weekly sessions.
2. Most churches offer the group several times throughout the year.
3. Women are encouraged to attend the support group as many times as they want.
4. It is advised for women going through the group more than once to use a new workbook each time. This will allow them to utilize the journal and writing portions fully without the distraction of their answers from the first time through.

THE IMPORTANCE OF PRAYER

Prayer is a key element of this study, and as the leader of the group it is important that you constantly cover your group in prayer.

You will want to begin praying for the women who will join your group long before the first meeting. Even if you don't know who they are, God knows and He is purposefully working behind the scenes to bring exactly the right women together.

You should be talking privately to God before, during, and after each meeting. Sometimes it seems daunting to lead a group of heartbroken women, but it is important to remember that God is the one who will give you what you need to be effective as the group leader. He is ultimately the one who is in charge of the group and you don't want to get in the way of what He might be trying to do. Therefore, be sure to invite God to be at the center of the group each week and ask Him to open up each person, including yourself, to what He wants you to hear, learn, and share.

You will also be praying aloud to open and close your group. It is perfectly fine to write out your prayer ahead of time if that will help you to feel more comfortable in praying in front of your group. As the weeks go by, you can rotate the opening and closing prayers among the group members, making sure never to put someone who may not be ready to pray aloud on the spot.

Leading a Grieving Moms, Finding Hope Group

BRINGING BIBLES

Throughout the GM study you will be using the Bible to teach, comfort, and inspire. There will be many opportunities to look up passages of Scripture as you seek God's Word on the various topics that will be covered. Some of the women in your group may be unfamiliar with the Bible and this is a great opportunity for them to begin to learn how to use it and where to find things within the pages.

Be sure to tell your group to bring their Bibles each week. It will be helpful to have a few extra Bibles available for anyone who doesn't bring one with them. You will also find all of the Scriptures used throughout the twelve-week group in the back of the workbook for quick reference.

HELPFUL HINTS FOR GM LEADERS

- Create a private FB page and label it "Grieving Moms – (then a name you'd like). Make sure to use the GM Logo on the banner of the FB Page.
- Encourage everyone to participate.
- Kay Warren's saying, "When you can you will" is a guiding principal in a GM group. Each woman will do things and participate when they can.
- It's okay if there are lulls in the conversation. Silence is important.
- You are a leader – not a teacher.
- Share your own story with your group – be vulnerable.
- Be sensitive to the different personalities in your group. Some will be quiet and shy, while others will be outgoing and talkative.
- The guidelines apply to you too!

GROUP ROSTER

There is a sheet for you to create a roster for your group in the back of the workbook. Each woman should have this information to help them keep in touch with each other during the week. This can be a valuable tool to help you keep track of who is showing up each week.

ATTENDANCE

It is a good idea to ask the women to text, email or call you if they won't be able to attend the group on any given week. When someone doesn't show up and you haven't heard from them, you should contact them the next day to check in with them. This helps them to know they are a valued member of the group, and that others are thinking about them and miss them when they don't attend. It will also help to "train" them to let you know ahead of time if they won't be there.

Purpose of the Edelweiss Flower

Found in the remotest parts of the Alps, the small white Edelweiss flower is the theme flower for the Grieving Moms, Find Hope program. Amidst the symbolic Landslide – the day that your child passed away – the Edelweiss is a reminder of life and hope to the Grieving Mom.

This German flower, whose name means noble and pure, flourishes in gorges, as if to fear no danger, holding its head high, its courage breaking through its winter prison of freezing snow and ice, drawn upward by the warmth of the sun. This ability to grow in harsh environments, surviving the roughest winters, is liken to the Grieving Moms, who have endured tremendous grief, pushing forward towards hope once again.

The Edelweiss grows on the highest and most inaccessible peaks near cliffs, teetering on the edge of the abyss, much like the Grieving Moms, devastated from loss, their souls inaccessible, unreachable, needing the warmth of others to bloom again.

Its double star formation, recognized as 'the birth flower,' is highly sought after, tempting those who desire it to go to great lengths and even fatal climbs to harvest this beautiful flower, to prove their love and devotion to those who'd receive it. So too, our gracious God goes to great lengths to prove His love and devotion to the Grieving Moms, seeking them out, giving them a second birth, leading them out of this Landslide into a new, yet different 'normal.'

You are the noble, courageous Edelweiss, Grieving Mom! God's prized possession, not forgotten, now accessible, ready to come to life once again.

At the highest point in the German Alps, Jacke discovers the resilient Edelweiss.

About the Authors

Jacke Van Woerkom

Certified Life Coach Jacke Van Woerkom is no stranger to personal trials, on January 15th, she faced the loss of her son due to suicide. Through her faith and the strength she found in her support community, Jacke gained a contagious spirit of hope, which she brings to others through speaking, coaching and workshops. Determined to see others succeed and find balance and purpose in the midst of life's darkest moments, Jacke serves as a lay counselor at Saddleback Community Church in Southern California. Her passionate heart reaches out towards other Grieving Moms who have suffered the loss of a child, creating opportunities for healing and helping them find hope through God

Sherry Lynn Ward

CEO of Square Tree Publishing and director of **Hurting Moms, Mending Hearts**, a support community of women, Sherry Ward is passionate about bringing hope to those who need it most. After years of battling a debilitating disease that plagued not only her, but both her sons, Sherry is determined to help others find purpose and healing in Christ. Author of **A Journey Out of the Wilderness**, her story of making sense out of life's struggles, Sherry is also a professor at several local Southern California colleges, using her eclectic background in business and counseling to equip others in their journey to find hope, healing, and restoration.

Table of Contents

Recommendations	i
Welcome Letter from Jacke	v
Acknowledgments	viii
Purpose of Grieving Moms, Finding Hope	x
About Jacke Van Woerkom and Sherry Lynn Ward	xvi
Support Group Elements	xviii
Group Guidelines	xxii
Resources	xxiv
Session 1 – Getting Started	1
Session 2 – Landslide Phase I – Frozen Phase	11
Session 3 – Landslide Phase II – Breakthrough Phase	23
Session 4 – Landslide Phase III – Look Up Phase	33
Session 5 – Trigger Events and Coping Skills	43
Session 6 – Family Dynamics	53
Session 7 – Forgiveness	65
Session 8 – Letting Go of our Child's Belongings	75
Session 9 – Dealing with Other People	83
Session 10 – Anniversaries, Birthdays, and Holidays	91
Session 11 – What We Have learned	101
Session 12 – Celebration of Hope and New Friends	109
Scriptures for Encouragement	117

Support Group Elements

WEEKLY FORMAT

Each week your meeting will contain certain elements and the flow will basically look the same from week to week. The women in your group will feel relaxed and comfortable coming each week when they know what format to expect.

OPENING PRAYER

Each weekly meeting will start with prayer. This helps us to clear our minds and to set aside the business of our day, as well as to open our hearts to what God wants us to hear and learn during our time together.

If you are uncomfortable praying aloud in front of a group, it is helpful to write your prayer out and read it during this time. Because of the potential diversity of your group (mature Christians, new Believers, non-Christians), it is not a good idea to call on anyone in the group to pray aloud unless you are certain that they are comfortable praying in a group and they have agreed to pray beforehand.

KEY SCRIPTURE

Every week Scripture will be used throughout the lesson as the basis or foundation of what we are learning. We will start each session with a key verse that is relevant to the week's topic of conversation.

In the back of the workbook you will find a listing of every Scripture referenced throughout the material. This will be a great resource for the women because they can refer to the verses even after the group is finished.

SHARING

Grieving Moms, Finding Hope provides a safe place to talk about the pain of losing a child. We know that everyone in the room is going through feelings and emotions similar to ours and that gives us the courage to open up with one another as we share our deepest hurts. By talking about our grieving process, we begin to experience freedom from the power it has had over us. It is a wonderful thing to realize that we are not the only mom who is going through the agony of losing a child. As we listen to other Grieving Moms tell their stories, we begin to find strength in the fact that we are not alone. Lifelong bonds and friendships are formed in this group and you are encouraged to share your contact information and to reach out to one another during the week.

Support Group Elements

The women in your group will be coming with many different situations relating to their personal Landslide. For some, sharing will come easily and they will open up immediately with the most intimate details of what is going on in their family. For others, it will be much more difficult to share. Some of them may have never told anyone the things they are being asked to share in the group, and it may take them a few weeks to trust the safety of the group enough to share more than on a superficial level. Be patient and allow each woman to share at her own pace as she feels ready.

It is also important to remember that listening to others plays a huge role in the process of healing. Many *Grieving Moms* feel that they are the only ones experiencing this kind of pain and sometimes the guilt and shame that goes along with the grief, but as they listen to the other moms share their stories they will realize that they are not alone.

It is not necessary for you, as the leader, to interject or offer advice as the women in your group share. You should be listening just like everyone else. God will show up and use each woman's sharing to touch others in the group in a different way. Let it happen!

VIDEO

Many Grieving Moms have received healing and hope by participating in a **Grieving Moms, Finding Hope** group. Some of them have recorded their experience in order to encourage you along this journey. Each week you will watch a short video segment of a Grieving Mom telling part of her story. As you hear their stories you will come to understand that you are not alone and that there is hope for you to once again experience peace and joy in your life.

You will notice the QR Code next to the video section in the GM book. By scanning these codes with your phone using a free downloadable mobile app, you and the women in your group will be able to access the videos at any time. This means that anyone who is absent on a given night will still be able to view the video. The videos are also available on *www.GrievingMoms.com*. The women in your group can view the videos multiple times or share them with their friends.

DISCUSSION

Each week we will be learning about different elements of being a Grieving Mom. We are all experiencing the loss of a child and the pain of grieving over that loss. As we make our way through this workbook we will begin to understand how to deal with our pain and grieve in a productive way that moves us forward through the process. You will be given tips and tools to help you heal from the grieve and to even find joy again in your life.

Support Group Elements

This is the actual "teaching" time of each group meeting where you will be presenting the new ideas in the material and encouraging the women to respond according to the suggestions along the way. Do not force a woman to participant, but allow her to engage when she is ready.

You can read the lesson to your group or have the women take turns reading. Feel free to be creative with the teaching, but be sure to cover everything that is written as each week is designed to be a stepping stone to the next week's material.

Quick Share

We highly encourage group participation, and through the Quick Share component, it gives the group an opportunity to share their experiences with the material that was just covered.

This is a quick interactive part of each session and it will help the women engage with the lesson and each other in a tangible way.

Spindrift Thoughts

A Spindrift Thought is a thought or emotion that is unstable and can cause us to drift back into unhealthy ways that do not lead us toward healing and is incapable of holding protection. We discuss the ways in which these thoughts can deter us in our healing journey.

The Spindrift Thoughts are a way for the moms to reveal some of the unhealthy ways they have been viewing their situation. Allow time for the moms to share their own thoughts during this section, and to read the Scripture for each thought.

Activity

We will take what we learn each week and apply it to our lives in some practical way and then share that with the group. These activities will deepen the experience and help you to find out where you are in your process and how to continue moving forward through your grief.

This is the interactive part of each session and it will help the women engage with the lesson and each other in a tangible way. It will also help to guide the direction of the sharing for the current week.

Support Group Elements

Moving Forward

Each week you will be given an activity to work on during the week in order to deepen your experience with the ideas that were shared. Although the Moving Forward activity is optional, it is <u>highly recommended</u> and designed to help you get to the next level of healing and hope.

Encourage your group members to engage in the Moving Forward activity on their own during the week. It can be helpful if you send out an email or text during the week to remind the moms about it and to cheer them on as they work on completing this part of the group on their own.

Closing Prayer

We will end each week by praying for requests and concerns that you may have and group members are encouraged to pray for each other throughout the week, through private Facebook pages or private group text messaging.

Spend a few minutes before the closing prayer asking for specific prayer requests. Let the women know that they can write each other's requests at the end of each session in the Prayer Request section.

If there is time you can pray for the individual requests or even have the moms pray for one another before you dismiss the group. You can encourage them to pray for each other and their special requests throughout the week.

Preview of Next Week

At the end of each session you will be given a quick overview of the discussion topic for the next week.

Be sure to look ahead so you will be prepared to tell the group what the topic will be for the next week.

At the bottom of the page you will see the page number. In parenthesis you will see another number. This number is the corresponding number in the GM Participant Guide so that the women can follow along with you.

Group Guidelines

> The guidelines should be read and explained in detail at the beginning of the first meeting. Let the women know that these guidelines are important in keeping the group a safe place to share. You may want to read them periodically at the beginning of subsequent meetings, especially if you notice that the group is struggling to adhere to one or more of them. Remember, one of your most important roles as the group leader is to maintain the guidelines.

🗝 Whatever is said or prayed about within the safety of our group will remain confidential with its members.

> It is critically important that this group is a safe place where everyone can feel free to express themselves without fear of judgment or that what they share will be talked about outside of the group. This includes women who are members of the group talking among themselves outside of the group about what someone else has shared. Remember, what is shared in the group stays in the group.

🗝 When someone else is speaking, listen without interrupting. This includes trying to comfort someone who is crying. There is healing in tears and we want to allow them to flow.

> Each woman should have the freedom to share without anyone else interjecting their own thoughts.

🗝 We are here to encourage, support, comfort, and uplift one another. We are not here to judge one another or fix each other. We bring no scales to the table.

> We want an atmosphere of encouragement in the group.

🗝 Although there will be times when it is necessary to be flexible, we will keep our sharing to a five (5) minute time limit to allow everyone an opportunity to share.

> This ensures that no one will be able to monopolize the time. There may be rare times that it is necessary to be flexible, but for the most part this guideline should be strictly adhered to.

Group Guidelines

🗝 You are encouraged to bring your Bible to the group as we will be going through Scriptures each week. The group leaders will have extra Bibles on hand in case you do not have one.

> **Since you will be going through Scriptures each week, you may want to have a few extra Bibles on hand in case anyone forgets to bring their Bible. Keep in mind some of the women may not be Christians, so make them feel welcomed and comfortable in the group.**

🗝 Group members are encouraged to continue their relationships with one another outside of the group.

> **We have provided a list at the back of the book for the *Grieving Moms* to put their information to keep in touch.**

Resources

Website
www.GrievingMoms.com

Email
info@GrievingMoms.com

Sign up for your daily encouraging words "Hope at Sunrise."

Jacke Van Woerkom has put together words of encouragement using some of the Scriptures that have inspired her along her journey as a Grieving Mom. She hopes that they will bring you comfort and peace as you go through each day.
Sign up at **www.GrievingMoms.com**

SISTER SUPPORT GROUP
- Hurting Moms, Mending Hearts www.hurtingmoms.com

RECOMMENDED READING
- A Journey Out of the Wilderness (book) by Sherry Lynn Ward
- A Journey Out of the Wilderness (blog) www.sherrylynnward.com
- The Story of a Hurting Mom (book) by Cathy Taylor
- A Grace Disguised (book) by Jerry Sittser
- Streams in the Desert (online devotional) – L.B. Cowman
- You'll Get Through This (book) by Max Lucado

RECOMMENDED WEBSITES
- www.GrievingMoms.com – For Hope in the Landslide
- www.HurtingMoms.com – For moms who are experiencing hurt over the choices and actions of their teen or adult children
- www.BlueLetterBible.org – For Bible verses and original language

COUNSELING
- SOZO – www.bethel.com/ministries/bethel-sozo-international

Getting Started

SESSION ONE

"It's okay – not to be okay."
Holly MacDonald
Grieving Mom, CA

The group leader may want to stand at the door to the meeting room and greet the women as they arrive. They will be somewhat nervous and apprehensive about being there and you can set the tone by giving them a warm welcome.

It is a good idea to provide name tags, at least for the first couple of weeks until the women get to know each other.

 ## OPENING PRAYER

The group leader should open the group in prayer. Remember, if you are not comfortable praying aloud yet you can write out a prayer ahead of time and read it.

 ## KEY SCRIPTURE

Though the mountains be shaken and the hills be removed, yet my unfailing love for you will not be shaken nor my covenant of peace be removed, says the Lord, who has compassion on you. Isaiah 54:10

They can refer to these Scriptures throughout the day for peace and comfort. Encourage the moms to carry them with them and to read them often so that these Scriptures will be impressed upon their hearts. We have GM Scripture Cards available in the Grieving Moms store at www.GrievingMoms.com.

 ## SHARING

This week you will meet the women in your group

Getting Started

WELCOME

As you welcome the *Grieving Moms* you will want to help them understand that they have come to the right place. This will give them some immediate relief from the anxiety they may be feeling.

Below is a suggestion of what to say as you welcome the women to your group. You can read it, paraphrase it in your own words, or welcome them in your own words from your heart.

God has purposefully brought us all together here today because we have a lost a child and we have all experienced a Landslide in our lives. We are in this support group because there is something very powerful about being in a safe place where we can share our stories and our pain as well as listen to others who are going through similar circumstances. Somehow by talking about our deepest hurt, it begins to lose the power that it has had over us and we find relief in being able to express ourselves without fear of being judged. As we listen to others in the group share their own experiences, we realize that we are not alone.

Today we start on a journey, a journey that will give our hearts hope again, and give us the tools to finally find peace and joy in our lives again. We will be referring to Scripture over and over again, so it is important that you to bring your Bibles each week.

VIDEO Coming soon.

"Grieving Moms, Finding Hope is all about getting out from under the Landslide. When my son committed suicide, I didn't think I could ever get out from under the Landslide, but God has shown me how to have peace and hope again despite my son's unexpected death." - Jacke Van Woerkom

By listening to some other *Grieving Moms* share their experience and what they learned in the GM support group, the women in your group will be encouraged. They will be able to relate to the women on the video because they are all *Grieving Moms*.

DISCUSSION
This week we will discuss different ways in which we handle our grief.

INTRODUCTIONS
Go around the room and have each woman introduce herself. You may want to provide name tags for the first few weeks until you get to know one another.

GUIDELINES
Read the guidelines found at the beginning of the workbook and briefly explain each one making sure that the women understand how important they are.

Getting Started

SPECIAL NOTE

Even in the midst of the landslide, God's covenant of peace will not be removed. During our time together, we will learn to have peace even in the midst of our grief and find hope in our situation. Through the *Grieving Moms* group we will develop lasting relationship with new friends who completely get what we are going through.

Quick Share

- What prompted you to connect with the **Grieving Moms, Finding Hope** group?
- Please feel free to share whatever you feel comfortable discussing.

    Remember, your story is important.

> **It is helpful if you share first, that way the other women will have time to compose their thoughts.**
>
> **Go around the room or table rather than wait for people to speak up at random. This will cut down on the time and ensure that everyone has the opportunity to share.**
>
> **Although it is fine for you to share your struggles with the group, it is also important that you find a way to offer hope through your sharing. Many of the women in your group are there because they feel that their situation is hopeless, and you want to encourage them that God will help them through this season of their lives and, most importantly, that there is hope for them and their family.**

DISCUSSION

Set Time Aside to Grieve

It is extremely important to grieve. If you don't grieve now, it will come up later in your life in unexpected ways. The important factor is not necessarily **how** you mourn, but that you **do** mourn. In our culture, people are not always expressive in grief and they tend to want you to 'get over' it quickly. But mourning takes time.

> *"Let time—have time."*
> Sherry Ward

Getting Started

Four Responses to our Grief
1. Not Moving
2. Moving Too Fast
3. Neutral
4. Moving Forward

NOT MOVING
- ▶ Feelings:
  - I don't deserve to come out
  - I don't deserve to be happy, while my child is not here
  - It feels more comfortable to just stay here
  - Subconsciously I want to punish myself for any part I may have played in their death

MOVING TOO FAST
- ▶ Feelings:
  - I don't like to feel this pain
  - I don't want to think about it
  - Pushing down feelings and denial
  - If I just keep myself busy, I won't have to deal with the pain

NEUTRAL
- ▶ Feelings:
  - I'm going through this, but I don't know how to get out
  - Stuck, but I want to come out
  - I'm not sure how to move forward
  - I'm not going backwards, but I'm not going forward

MOVING FORWARD
- ▶ Feelings:
  - I fully feel the grief, but want to come out
  - I'm willing to move forward to find healing
  - I have a good support system to help me
  - I have the tools necessary to help me get out

Circle some of the statements above that you resonate with.
Share with the group.

Getting Started

◉ Moving Forward

It is our goal to equip you with the tools and find the friendships that will carry you through this grieving process. Each week you will be given a Moving Forward assignment to work on that week. There is no pressure to do all of them, however we highly encourage you to do as many of them as possible to enable you to continue moving forward in your process of healing.

These are some ways you can move forward this week.
- Read the Scriptures on the following page aloud this week.
- Journal - Journaling is a great way to express how you are feeling on paper and can be a very freeing exercise. Select one or two Scriptures and write them down in your Moving Forward journal and then mediate on them this week.

Supporting Each Other

Here are some ways to stay in touch with your group throughout the week.

We highly recommend you encourage each other during the week.
- Exchange contact info on the form in the back of the book
- Start a group text
- Start a Private GM Facebook Page

Although the Moving Forward element of the group is optional, encourage the women in your group to choose and engage in at least one of the suggestions given. Explain that the healing and growth will happen sooner if they are spending time during the week utilizing the tools they are being given.

◉ Closing Prayer

One of the most powerful aspects a of GM support group is the fact that women are praying for other moms and for their family. Be sure to emphasize this as you finish up the meeting.

◉ Preview of Next Week

Landslide Phase I – Frozen Phase
Next week we will be discussing the first phase of our Landslide called the Frozen Phase.

Be sure to look ahead so you will be prepared to tell the group what the topic will be for the next week.

Encouraging Scriptures

These are some Scriptures that will comfort and encourage you. The Word of God gives us hope even when we feel helpless and hopeless in our situation. I encourage you to read these and other passages throughout the week.

Though the mountains be shaken and the hills be removed, yet my unfailing love for you will not be shaken nor my covenant of peace be removed,' says the Lord, who has compassion on you. Isaiah 54:10

We are hard pressed on every side, but not crushed; perplexed, but not in despair; persecuted, but not abandoned; struck down, but not destroyed. We always carry around in our body the death of Jesus, so that the life of Jesus may also be revealed in our body. 2 Corinthians 4:8-10

And now, here's what I'm going to do: I'm going to start all over again. I'm taking her back out into the wilderness where we had our first date, and I'll court her. I'll give her bouquets of roses. I'll turn Heartbreak Valley into Acres of Hope. Hosea 2:14-15a (MSG)

The LORD is near to the brokenhearted and saves the crushed in spirit. Psalm 34:18 (ESV)

He heals the brokenhearted and binds up their wounds. Psalm 147:3 (ESV)

For this child I prayed, and the Lord has granted me my petition that I made to him. Therefore I have lent him to the Lord. As long as he lives, he is lent to the Lord. And he worshiped the Lord there. 1 Samuel 1:27-28 (ESV)

Blessed are those who mourn, for they shall be comforted. Matthew 5:4 (ESV)

And regarding the question, friends, that has come up about what happens to those already dead and buried, we don't want you in the dark any longer. First off, you must not carry on over them like people who have nothing to look forward to, as if the grave were the last word. Since Jesus died and broke loose from the grave, God will most certainly bring back to life those who died in Jesus. And then this: We can tell you with complete confidence—we have the Master's Word on it—that when the Master comes again to get us, those of us who are still alive will not get a jump on the dead and leave them behind. In actual fact, they'll be ahead of us. The Master himself will give the command. Archangel thunder! God's trumpet blast! He'll come down from heaven and the dead in Christ will rise—they'll go first. Then the rest of us who are still alive at the time will be caught up with them into the clouds to meet the Master. Oh, we'll be walking on air! And then there will be one huge family reunion with the Master. So, reassure one another with these words. I Thessalonians 4:13-17 (MSG)

Encouraging Scriptures

Who comforts us in all our affliction, so that we may be able to comfort those who are in any affliction, with the comfort with which we ourselves are comforted by God. 2 Corinthians 1:4 (ESV)

It is the L<small>ORD</small> who goes before you. He will be with you; he will not leave you or forsake you. Do not fear or be dismayed. Deuteronomy 31:8 (ESV)

When they arrive at the gates of death, G<small>OD</small> welcomes those who love him. Oh, G<small>OD</small>, here I am, your servant, your faithful servant: set me free for your service! I'm ready to offer the thanksgiving sacrifice and pray in the name of G<small>OD</small>. Psalm 116:14-17 (MSG)

Behold, the dwelling place of God is with man. He will dwell with them, and they will be his people, and God himself will be with them as their God. He will wipe away every tear from their eyes, and death shall be no more, neither shall there be mourning, nor crying, nor pain anymore, for the former things have passed away. And he who was seated on the throne said, Behold, I am making all things new. Also he said, Write this down, for these words are trustworthy and true. Revelation 21:3b-5 (ESV)

Your eyes saw my unformed substance; in your book were written, every one of them, the days that were formed for me, when as yet there was none of them. Psalm 139:16 (ESV)

For I know the plans I have for you, declares the L<small>ORD</small>, plans for welfare and not for evil, to give you a future and a hope. Jeremiah 29:11 (ESV)

To the choirmaster: according to The Doe of the Dawn. A Psalm of David. My God, my God, why have you forsaken me? Why are you so far from saving me, from the words of my groaning? O my God, I cry by day, but you do not answer, and by night, but I find no rest. Yet you are holy, enthroned on the praises of Israel. In you our fathers trusted; they trusted, and you delivered them. To you they cried and were rescued; in you they trusted and were not put to shame. Psalm 22:1-8 (ESV)

He will wipe away every tear from their eyes, and death shall be no more, neither shall there be mourning, nor crying, nor pain anymore, for the former things have passed away. Revelation 21:4 (ESV)

Since therefore the children share in flesh and blood, he himself likewise partook of the same things, that through death he might destroy the one who has the power of death, that is, the devil. Hebrews 2:14 (ESV)

Moving Forward Journal

Pick a Scripture(s) that spoke to your heart.
_____
_____
_____
_____
_____
_____
_____
_____

What did this verse(s) mean to you?
_____
_____
_____
_____
_____
_____
_____
_____
_____
_____
_____
_____
_____
_____
_____
_____
_____

Prayer Requests

Name:_____

Situation: _____

_____

_____

_____

Name:_____

Situation: _____

_____

_____

_____

Name:_____

Situation: _____

_____

_____

_____

Name:_____

Situation: _____

_____

_____

_____

Name:_____

Situation: _____

_____

_____

_____

Landslide Phase 1 – Frozen Phase

SESSION TWO

"Busyness is redefined when tragedy freezes time."
Jacke Van Woerkom

These next three sessions deal with the different phases of pain and grief we experience in our Landslide. We divided this section into three sessions because there is potentially so much to talk about.

OPENING PRAYER

KEY SCRIPTURE

We are pressed on every side by troubles, but we are not crushed. We are perplexed, but not driven to despair...we get knocked down, but we are not destroyed. 2 Corinthians 4:8-9 (NLT)

SHARING

Share one of the Scriptures that really stood out to you last week.

VIDEO Coming soon.

Encourage the women to elaborate on which verse they selected and how it spoke to them and gave them hope. The moms will be encouraged by listening to one another and it will help them understand different perspectives.

DISCUSSION

We will be discussing the Frozen Phase and what that looks like in our process of healing.

In these next few sessions, there is a lot of material. Have the women read it before they come to the group - that way they will be familiar with the material ahead of time.

The lesson can be read in several ways. You can read it to the group, you can ask for a volunteer to read it, or you can split it up and have several women read.

The purpose of each lesson is to direct the focus of the group so that they are not getting "stuck" on one element of being a Grieving Mom, but are actually progressing in the process of grieving.

Landslide Phase 1 – Frozen Phase

OUR CURRENT PHASE OF PAIN AND GRIEF

The pain we are experiencing is caused by many factors:

- Replaying the day of the Landslide in your mind over and over
- Feeling like you are somehow responsible for their death
- You and your spouse do not understand each other's grief
- The "if onlys" creep into our thoughts on a regular basis
- We feel helpless to move forward
- Feeling like this will never end

➔ Circle the ones above that apply to you. Share with the group.

> Have the women share their answers with the group. The Quick Share activity is meant to break up the sessions into smaller parts and to help the women engage and share.

What is a Phase?
A phase is a period of time during which a person behaves in a particular way, with the goal of transitioning out of that phase at the right time.

Transitioning Through the Phases
As we begin to realize that our child is not coming back, we feel tremendous loss and we can't move on in our own lives until we go through a process of grieving for what was and what might have been. This process has several phases, but it is important to interpret these phases loosely. There is not an orderly progression from one phase to the next and it is common for us to experience the phases out of order, have them repeat themselves, or even to have multiple phases hit at the same time.

The important thing to remember is that it is perfectly normal to grieve for the sense of loss we are experiencing regarding our child and we need to allow ourselves the space to do so.

We want you to have the freedom to grieve in your own way and through the phases that best meet your needs at any given time. If we view them in chronological order, it gives the false expectation that we only go through them once, when in fact it is more of an ebb and flow through the phases.

Landslide Phase 1 – Frozen Phase

Transitioning Tips

- √ Share and grieve right where you are
- √ There is no right or wrong way to grieve
- √ May go in and out of phases
- √ Phases may come back in unexpected places
- √ Be open to moving through your grief

FROZEN PHASE

- The Landslide hits!
- Received the news that our child has passed away.
- Immobilized, barely able to move or breathe.
- Take life one minute, one hour, one day at a time.
- Time stands still.

When something is frozen, it's just that...frozen. It's lifeless and just sits there and time stands still. God's design when these landslides come down, is to protect our hearts and minds. We enter into a place of numbness and denial to prevent any further mental or physical injury. The more dramatic or severe the situation, the greater the shock and the longer we become paralyzed and numb.

Landslide Phase 1 – Frozen Phase

REACTIONS

Blindsided
- The news came as a complete shock
- Denial - "No this didn't happen!"
- Numb
- Hopeless
- Withdraw from those around us

Dazed and Confused
- Thinking is disoriented
- Unable to make decisions
- Overwhelmed and unable to move

Anxiety
- We may feel panic
- Sleeplessness
- Irrational thoughts
- Suicidal thoughts

Fear
- Take control over situations around you
- Protect ourselves
- Refuse help
- Make quick decisions too fast

Quick Share

Share with the group any of these emotions you have been experiencing.

> **This is a time to allow the women to share with one another. Make sure this is a safe place to share with no judgement about how the women are feeling. As the leader make sure to set this non-judgmental tone in the group.**

Landslide Phase 1 – Frozen Phase

What are Spindrift Thoughts?
Spindrift is a loose, powder snow incapable of holding protection.[1]
A Spindrift Thought is a thought or emotion that is unstable and can cause us to drift back into unhealthy ways that do not lead us toward healing and is incapable of holding protection.

"I'll take my life because then I'll see my child again soon."
The Lord himself goes before you and will be with you; he will never leave you nor forsake you. Do not be afraid; do not be discouraged. Deuteronomy 31:8

"What did I do to make this happen?"
The accuser of our brothers, who accuses them before our God day and night, has been hurled down. Revelation 12:10

"Why do bad things happen to good people?"
No weapon that is fashioned against you shall succeed, and you shall confute every tongue that rises against you in judgment. This is the heritage of the servants of the Lord and their vindication from me, declares the Lord. Isaiah 54:17

"I will never feel joy ever again."
Why are you downcast, O my soul? Why so disturbed within me? Put your hope in God, for I will yet praise him, my Savior and my God. Psalm 42:5

"People are going to judge our family!"
Therefore judge nothing before the appointed time; wait till the Lord comes. He will bring to light what is hidden in darkness and will expose the motives of men's hearts. At that time each will receive his praise from God. 1 Corinthians 4:5

Share with the group any Spindrift Thoughts you have on a reoccurring basis.

---

[1] http://santiamalpineclub.org/mountain/climbing/terms/

Landslide Phase 1 – Frozen Phase

SITTING SHIVA

The word "Shiva" is Hebrew for the word "seven". When someone in the Jewish culture has lost a loved one, many will visit and sit with them during this seven-day period. This is known as 'Sitting Shiva."

Family and friends come to their house. It is a not a time to entertain those that are there, but your family and friends bring food to your house so that you do not have to be out in the public yet. It allows you a safe place to isolate and mourn through your grief.

During this time of being with friends and family:
- Communicate what you're going through
- Don't be afraid to ask for what you need
- Give yourself grace and have realistic expectations

ISOLATING vs. INSOLATING

Insulating is different than isolating. To insulate is to protect from the outside through the love of others, while to isolate is to have no contact with others at all for extended periods of time.

Ask the Holy Spirit to insulate you like a cocoon during this time and so envelop you with His love that you are fully protected during this vulnerable time.

Landslide Phase 1 – Frozen Phase

 **Activity**

Discuss ways in which you have either isolated or insolated in your process of grieving.

List some things that helped you during this phase?

_____
_____
_____
_____
_____
_____
_____
_____
_____
_____
_____
_____
_____
_____
_____
_____
_____
_____
_____
_____

Landslide

I was there...
when the Landslide hit
frozen in despair
not knowing where to turn
gasping for air.
I saw you in your pain.

I was there...
avalanche of emotions
buried beneath the snow
hope held prisoner
nowhere to go.
I was there in your pain.

I was there...
on that memorial day
present but not there
wanting to be anywhere else
life just wasn't fair.
I carried you that day.

I was there...
in sleepless nights and ugly cries
as you yelled out, Why?
the pain too great to bear
Why my child? Why did he die?
I held you that day.

I was there...
as life went on
alone, but not alone
tide high—tide low
new normal digging through the unknown.
I hugged you that day.

I was there...
counting the days
Father Time like a taunting clock
each stroke a past reminder
triggers being unlocked.
I held eternity that day.

I was there...
as you resurfaced
breaking through
the ordinary, not so ordinary
not knowing what to do.
I let you 'just be' that day.

I was there...
first anniversary — first birthday
baby pictures forever hung in your heart
wanting just to speak your name
memories needing a new start.
I remembered you that day.

I was there...
when days turned to years
letting go of your child's things
wanting to hang on
unsure of what the next day brings.
I helped you let go.

I was there...
the day you asked, "Why?"
completely perplexed
now the new question...
"What's next?"
I gave you hope that day.

I am here...
with your son who is in Heaven
counting down the days to see
that final hour I call you home
he'll be sitting next to me.
I have resurrection power.

Sherry Lynn Ward
Reprinted by permission.
The Landslide, Sherry Lynn Ward
© 2017, Square Tree Publishing
All rights reserved.
www.sherrylynnward.com

Landslide Phase 1 – Frozen Phase

◎ Moving Forward

Spend some time thinking about the Frozen Phase.

- What positive steps have you taken or can take as you move through this phase?

- Which Spindrift Thoughts are you stuck in?
  Meditate on the Scriptures that you resonated with.

> **Encourage the women to do the Moving Forward activity each week. These activities will help them move forward in their healing. However, if a woman just can't bring herself to do it, then that is okay. We all will grieve and heal at our own pace.**

◎ Closing Prayer

◎ Preview of Next Week

Landslide Phase II – Breakthrough Phase
Next week we will talk about the next phase of grief and where we are in our journey.

Moving Forward Journal

What positive steps have you taken or can take as you move through this phase?
___

Prayer Requests

Name:_____
Situation: _____
_____
_____
_____

Name:_____
Situation: _____
_____
_____
_____

Name:_____
Situation: _____
_____
_____
_____

Name:_____
Situation: _____
_____
_____
_____

Name:_____
Situation: _____
_____
_____
_____

Landslide Phase 2 – Breakthrough Phase

SESSION THREE

"God is not doing the next thing, He is doing a new thing."
Christine Caine

Some of the women may already be past the Frozen Phase, while some may still be in that phase. Encourage the women through their process of grief. Remember – when they can, they will.

OPENING PRAYER

KEY SCRIPTURE

See, I am doing a new thing! Now it springs up; do you not perceive it?
Isaiah 43:19a

SHARING

Which Scriptures were you able to meditate on this week that helped you?

This is basically a recap of the last session and an opportunity for the moms to share about the Moving Forward work that they have done during the week. Directing the sharing toward something specific helps to keep the group on track for moving ahead in the healing process.

VIDEO

Coming soon.

DISCUSSION

We will be discussing the Breakthrough Phase and what that looks like in our process of healing.

Landslide Phase 2 - Breakthrough Phase

SPECIAL REMINDER

As we go through the phases, we want you to have the freedom to grieve in the way that best meets your needs. There is no right or wrong way to grieve. There is no right or wrong way to process that grief through the phases. Find the freedom in this GM support group to share and grieve right where you are, but be open to moving through the grief so that you are not stuck there longer than necessary.

> This is a very important reminder, so make sure you read it to the women in your group.

Transitioning Tips
- √ Share and grieve right where you are
- √ There is no right or wrong way to grieve
- √ May go in and out of phases
- √ Phases may come back in unexpected places
- √ Be open to moving through your grief

Landslide Phase 2 - Breakthrough Phase

BREAKTHROUGH PHASE
- Our face breaks through the frozen snow
- We gasp, taking in that first breath of air
- We see and feel the warmth of family and friends telling us, "We're here for you."
- Exhaustion and reality also surface

We slowly peak out from under the Landslide, the adrenaline necessary to breathe beneath in our Frozen Phase minimizes. We are weak and weary to participate in the world around us as we try to find life again. It requires so much to keep warm when we are in the Frozen Phase. Once thawed, our heart begins beating again, however, we may return to the impact of the Landslide.

HERE'S WHERE IT IS IMPORTANT NOT TO ISOLATE!

SEARCH AND RESCUE TEAM
Find people who will be your Search and Rescue team. A Search and Rescue (S&R) team are people in your life that are a safe place where you can share freely and know that you will get the support and encouragement that you need. Continue to be insulated in God's promises and be with these people God sent as your Search and Rescue team.

This S&R team may be some of the same friends we have had for a long time, however, it may be some new friends that God sends our way, especially in the GM support group. Some of us may have been sad to see some of our most trusted friends not there for us. We may even have to grieve over the loss of their friendship. They just may not be equipped with the tools to help us in this phase of the process and that is okay. Look to this new S&R team to be there through this phase.

HELPFUL IDEA
We may know other people who can pray for us from a distance. One of the Grieving Moms in the community wrote a letter about her son's passing and then when someone would ask her about it, she'd simply gave the letter to them. This way she did not have go over the details of her child's passing if she did not feel up to it.

Share if your friends have been there for you or you need to develop a new S&R Team.

Landslide Phase 2 - Breakthrough Phase

DRAMATICALLY DIFFERENT

Above the Landslide, we view life as we once knew it, dramatically different. We attempt to venture out to perform normal tasks taking one step at a time.

Life greets us in these places with, "Hi, (insert name), how are you?"

In that moment, we want to let it all out and tell our story, but do other people desire to hear our new truth? Do they truly care? Can they handle our story?

There is a beautiful chaos all around us as family and friends assemble efforts to restore hope back into our lives with prayer, cards, and meals. You may feel alone, but not alone.

REACTIONS

Awareness

- This is my reality
- Alone, but never alone
- Every step I take feels different

Scared

- Directionless
- Panicky thoughts
- Fearful

Share with the group any of these emotions you have felt in this phase.

Landslide Phase 2 – Breakthrough Phase

Spindrift Thoughts

"What do I do now?"
All of the things that we needed to do after our Landslide are now done, but we are at a loss at what to do next. Spend some time with God. It is not about doing, but about being with God. Go easy on yourself and don't worry if you are not doing a lot of things, and be careful not to isolate too much from your S&R team.

Are you tired? Worn out? Burned out on religion? Come to me. Get away with me and you'll recover your life. I'll show you how to take a real rest. Walk with me and work with me—watch how I do it. Learn the unforced rhythms of grace. I won't lay anything heavy or ill-fitting on you. Keep company with me and you'll learn to live freely and lightly. Matthew 11:28-30 (MSG)

I'm not saying that I have this all together, that I have it made. But I am well on my way, reaching out for Christ, who has so wondrously reached out for me. Philippians 3:12 (MSG)

"Why didn't I...?" "Why did he/she...?"
The definition of blame is taking responsibility for a fault or wrong. We may have thoughts that are not from God that say, "If you only did this, then that would not have happened." Or, "Why didn't I go and get him help sooner!?"

It is not your fault and the enemy would love to bring those accusing voices to your mind to tell you that you were to blame. BUT that simply is <u>NOT</u> true.

Then I heard a strong voice out of Heaven saying, Salvation and power are established! Kingdom of our God, authority of his Messiah! The Accuser of our brothers and sisters thrown out, who accused them day and night before God. They defeated him through the blood of the Lamb and the bold word of their witness. Revelation 12:10 (MSG)

For God did not send his Son into the world to condemn the world, but in order that the world might be saved through him. John 3:17 (ESV)

God met me more than halfway, he freed me from my anxious fears. Look at him; give him your warmest smile. Never hide your feelings from him. Psalm 34:4-5 (MSG)

Landslide Phase 2 – Breakthrough Phase

"I <u>need</u>….and I <u>have</u> to have…"

This is your Father you are dealing with, and he knows better than you what you need. With a God like this loving you, can pray very simply. Like this:
Our Father in heaven,
Reveal who you are.
Set the world right;
Do what's best—
as above, so below.
Keep us alive with three square meals.
Keep us forgiven with you and forgiving others.
Keep us safe from ourselves and the Devil.
You're in charge!
You can do anything you want!
You're ablaze in beauty!
Yes. Yes. Yes.
Matthew 6:8-13 (MSG)

"I know I will be judged!"

Sometimes we may feel like we are wearing a big Scarlet Letter A on our shirt. Not everyone will understand your situation, but that is okay. Stay with those friends on your Search and Rescue Team so that you get the support you need.

My beloved friends, let us continue to love each other since love comes from God. Everyone who loves is born of God and experiences a relationship with God. The person who refuses to love doesn't know the first thing about God, because God is love—so you can't know him if you don't love. I John 4:7-8 (MSG)

But they will have to give account to him who is ready to judge the living and the dead.
1 Peter 4:5

Landslide Phase 2 – Breakthrough Phase

◎ Activity

Share with the group any Spindrift Thoughts you have experienced on a reoccurring basis.
This will give you a clue of any areas in which you are stuck.
Write down the corresponding Scriptures and mediate on them this week.

◎ Moving Forward

- Find some people who will be on your Search and Rescue team.
- Choose people that are safe and will encourage you through this process.
- How has your S&R team encouraged you this week?

Note: You may have life-long friends you leave off this list because they are not a good fit for this season of your life. That is okay!

> **Let the women know that some of their life-long friends may not know how to be there for them in this season or may completely leave. During this time, new friends may emerge that are better suited to help them during this time in their life.**

◎ Closing Prayer

◎ Preview of Next Week

Landslide Phase III – Look Up Phase
Next week we will talk about the next phase of grief and where we are at in our journey.

Moving Forward Journal

- Find some people who will be on your Search and Rescue team.
- Choose people that are safe and will encourage you through this process.

Note: You may have life-long friends you leave off this list, because they are not a good fit for this season of your life. That is okay!

1. _____
2. _____
3. _____
4. _____
5. _____
6. _____
7. _____
8. _____
9. _____
10. _____

How have your Search and Rescue team encouraged you this week?
_____
_____
_____
_____
_____
_____
_____
_____
_____
_____
_____
_____
_____
_____
_____

Prayer Requests

Name:_____
Situation: _____
_____
_____
_____

Name:_____
Situation: _____
_____
_____
_____

Name:_____
Situation: _____
_____
_____
_____

Name:_____
Situation: _____
_____
_____
_____

Name:_____
Situation: _____
_____
_____
_____

Look Up Phase

SESSION FOUR

"Those on top of the mountain did not fall there."
Jacke Van Woerkom

Some of the women may still be in the previous two phases and may not be ready for this phase yet. That is okay. Encourage the women through their process of grief. Remember – when they can, they will.

OPENING PRAYER

KEY SCRIPTURE

I'm not saying that I have this all together, that I have it made. But I am well on my way, reaching out for Christ, who has so wondrously reached out for me…I've got my eye on the goal, where God is beckoning us onward—to Jesus…and I'm not turning back.
Philippians 3:12-14 (MSG)

SHARING

Were you able to identify who is on your Search and Rescue team? Share some of the ways they encouraged you this week.

VIDEO

Coming soon.

DISCUSSION

We will be discussing the Look Up Phase and what that looks like in our process of healing.

Look Up Phase

SPECIAL REMINDER

As we go through the phases, we want you to have the freedom to grieve in the way that best meets your needs. There is no right or wrong way to grieve. There is no right or wrong way to process that grief through the phases. Find the freedom in this GM support group to share and grieve right where you are, but be open to moving through the grief so that you are not stuck there for longer than necessary.

> **This is an important reminder to tell the women, even though you told them in the previous weeks. It will help to give them freedom to do what they can – where they are at in the process.**

Transitioning Tips
- √ Share and grieve right where you are
- √ There is no right or wrong way to grieve
- √ May go in and out of phases
- √ Phases may come back in unexpected places
- √ Be open to moving through your grief

Look Up Phase

LOOK UP PHASE

- I am doing my best to accept the fact that my child is no longer here
- Looking toward the future for the first time
- There is life after losing my precious child
- It is God's will that I move forward through the natural phases of grief in order to experience His healing power
- I am still needed by my other children/grandchildren, spouse, family, friends, or ministry

You have broken through the icy Landslide. It appears *insurmountable*! Now the question becomes: "What's next?" Can I go on without my child? In the Look Up phase, as you seek God, the narrative and the questions begin to change.

When your Landslide hit your question was:
"Why, God?"

Now in this phase your question becomes:
"What do I do with this, God?"

In the Look Up Phase, we are working through the fact that our child is no longer here. We have asked the question over and over, "Why, God?" – BUT a new question begins to emerge…"What do I do with this, God?" How will you turn this around for good?

In this phase, we may begin to accept the fact that our child is no longer here. This thought brings insecurity, sadness, and finally, acceptance. There may be thoughts you will need to push through. Thoughts that you are not to blame for your child's death, nor could you have prevented it by having done something different. God wants you to begin to move through these natural phases of grief in order to experience His healing power.

Quick Share

Share with your group where you are at in your process of healing.
Are you at the "Why, God" stage? Or the "What do I do with this, God?"

Look Up Phase

REACTIONS

Insecurity
- Confidence jolted
- Unsure if you are capable
- Resort to past patterns of handling challenges

Acceptance
- Respond to "What do I do with this, God?"
- Receive God's new direction
- React to the hope of your future

Quick Share

Share with the group any of these emotions you have felt in this phase.

Spindrift Thoughts

"I have no idea how I'm going to do this!"
Trust, Scripture, and prayer are keys that will help you through this next process. Trust that God will turn all things around for good. Stay in prayer and listen to what you feel He is telling you. Take it day by day.

I'll be with you as you do this, day after day after day, right up to the end of the age.
Matthew 28:20b (MSG)

If you don't know what you're doing, pray to the Father. He loves to help. You'll get his help, and won't be condescended to when you ask for it. Ask boldly, believingly, without a second thought.
James 1:5-6a (MSG)

God's Spirit is right alongside helping us along. If we don't know how or what to pray, it doesn't matter. He does our praying in and for us, making prayer out of our wordless sighs, our aching groans. He knows us far better than we know ourselves...and keeps us present before God. That's why we can be so sure that every detail in our lives of love for God is worked into something good.
Romans 8:26b-28 (MSG)

Look Up Phase

"This isn't fair!"

Many times we cry out to God that He is unfair. We question why we had to go through this Landslide as we were serving Him, while others seem unscathed by life when they are not even following Him. We may never get the why, but trust is the key that will unlock every door in our lives. Continue to trust God even when life doesn't make sense.

> *No doubt about it! God is good—good to good people, good to the good-hearted. But I nearly missed it, missed seeing his goodness. I was looking the other way...*
> *What's going on here? Is God out to lunch? Nobody's tending the store. The wicked get by with everything; they have it made, piling up riches; I've been stupid to play by the rules; what has it gotten me? A long run of bad luck, that's what—a slap in the face every time I walk out the door. If I'd have given in and talked like this, I would have betrayed your dear children...(Then) I entered the sanctuary of God. Then I saw the whole picture...I'm still in your presence, but you've taken my hand. You wisely and tenderly lead me, and then you bless me. You're all I want in heaven! You're all I want on earth! When my skin sags and my bones get brittle, God is rock-firm and faithful...I'm in the very presence of God—oh, how refreshing it is! I've made Lord God my home. God, I'm telling the world what you do!*
> Psalm 73:1-4, 11-16, 20-28 (MSG)

> *God is a safe place to hide, ready to help when we need him. We stand fearless at the cliff-edge of doom, courageous in sea storm and earthquake, Before the rush and roar of oceans, the tremors that shift mountains. Jacob-wrestling God fights for us, God-of-Angel-Armies protects us.*
> Psalm 46:1-3 (MSG)

"What is next?"

We have now come to realize that life will never be the same—but now what? We need to keep moving forward. God doesn't ask us to take ten steps forward and have the entire plan laid out ahead of time. He only asks us to take one step at a time. Do what gives you peace as the next step in your healing. Each person is different and each person's next step will vary, but as long you are moving forward, then it is good.

> *When I said, 'My foot is slipping,' your unfailing love, Lord, supported me. When anxiety was great within me, your consolation brought me joy.* Psalm 94-18-19

> *I'll show up and take care of you as I promised and bring you back home. I know what I'm doing. I have it all planned out—plans to take care of you, not abandon you, plans to give you the future you hope for.* Jeremiah 29:10b-11 (MSG)

Look Up Phase

"God you chose the wrong woman to do this, I will surely fail you!"

I remember God speaking to me one day in prayer and He said, "You are stronger than you know!" He repeated it to me three times and I thought to myself, 'What is He talking about?" Then the thought came…"Oh no, what is coming that I need to be so strong for?" Three months later one of my sons ended up in the hospital having seven different surgical procedures. I would have never thought I could have handled all that I went through, but I am a stronger woman today because of it. God never originates these Landslides, but He does use them for our benefit if we trust Him through the process. You are stronger than you know! (Sherry Ward)

This is what the Lord says: 'When people fall down, do they not get up? When someone turns away, do they not return?' Jeremiah 8:4

Whatever I have, wherever I am, I can make it through anything in the One who makes me who I am. Philippians 4:13 (MSG)

Quick Share

Share with the group any Spindrift Thoughts you have experienced on a reoccurring basis.
This will help you recognize any of the areas in which you are stuck.
Write down the corresponding Scriptures and mediate on them this week.

Activity

Sometimes these Spindrift Thoughts can gain a foothold and become lies that we believe. One way to cancel those lies is to begin to say the opposite in a declaration aloud over yourself. It doesn't matter if you believe them or not at the beginning, just make a habit of saying them every day and watch how things will begin to shift in your life.

> **Have the women read these next declarations aloud as a group. I want you to feel how the atmosphere in the room shifts as the women say their declarations aloud. Stress to them the importance of saying declarations and how it shifts the atmosphere around them. (Proverbs 18:21)**

Look Up Phase

Directions:
Read these declarations aloud together. Feel the power in the room that comes from your declarations.
   This is God's truth for you:
   - ✯ **The Truth is God will make me whole again.**
   - ✯ **The Truth is there is life after losing my child.**
   - ✯ **The Truth is I am still here.**
   - ✯ **The Truth is I am still needed by other people in my life, whether I can see it or not right now.**
   - ✯ **The Truth is my other children/grandchildren need me, my spouse needs me, and my family and friends need me.**
   - ✯ **The Truth is I still have a purpose here on earth to accomplish, while I am still here.**
   - ✯ **The Truth is God heals me when I share my pain with others.**

For the more we suffer for Christ, the more God will shower us with his comfort through Christ. Even when we are weighed down with troubles, it is for your comfort and salvation! For when we ourselves are comforted, we will certainly comfort you. Then you can patiently endure the same things we suffered. We are confident that as you share in our sufferings, you will also share in the comfort God gives us. 2 Corinthians 1:5-6

◎ Moving Forward

Go through the Scripture verses in this session and select three of them that resonate with you.

- Write down the declarations that we said aloud on a piece of paper and post it up in your house.
- Begin to say them daily even if you don't fully believe them yet.
- How has this begun to shift things in your life?
- Bring them with you to share next week.

> **The power of the declaration is in saying it aloud, even if the women still can't 'believe' it yet. Have the women continue saying their declarations despite their feeling or not fully believing it yet. The mouth goes first, and the heart will follow.**

◎ Closing Prayer

◎ Preview of Next Week
Trigger Events and Coping Skills
We will be discussing trigger events and some tools on how to cope.

Moving Forward Journal

What Scriptures verses resonated with you? Write them down.

1. _____
_____
_____
_____

2. _____
_____
_____
_____

3. _____
_____
_____
_____

DECLARATIONS

→ Write down the declarations that we said aloud on a piece of paper and post it up in your house.
→ Begin to say them daily even if you don't fully believe them yet.
→ How has this begun to shift things in your life?

_____
_____
_____
_____
_____
_____
_____
_____
_____
_____
_____

Prayer Requests

Name:_____

Situation: _____

_____

_____

_____

Name:_____

Situation: _____

_____

_____

_____

Name:_____

Situation: _____

_____

_____

_____

Name:_____

Situation: _____

_____

_____

_____

Name:_____

Situation: _____

_____

_____

_____

Trigger Events and Coping Skills

SESSION FIVE

*"Two words will help you cope
when you run low on hope: accept and trust."*
Charles Swindoll

This session is focused on trigger events and coping skills. For some of the women, they may confess unhealthy coping skills they have been doing. Continue to create a non-judgmental environment in the group, as they are transparent and honest with their actions.

OPENING PRAYER

KEY SCRIPTURE

Do not be anxious about anything, but in everything by prayer and supplication with thanksgiving let your requests be made known to God. And the peace of God, which surpasses all understanding, will guard your hearts and your minds in Christ Jesus. Philippians 4:7 (ESV)

SHARING

Share the Scriptures that you wrote down as well as the declarations that you said aloud this week.

VIDEO

Coming soon.

DISCUSSION

We will be discussing Trigger Events and some tools on how to cope.

Trigger Events and Coping Skills

TRIGGER EVENTS

Trigger Events are things that set off a memory tape or flashback transporting the person back to the event of their original trama.[2]

Triggers may cause anxiety, fear, or panic as the scene is repeated and you are taken back to that devastating memory. It may cause unhealthy reactions before you even realize that you are upset.

Being aware that you may have a trigger is the first step in helping to overcome the corresponding behavior. Trigger Events can be based on sight, smell, sound, touch or taste.

Sample Triggers
- Photos, cards, letters, e-mail
- Phone Rings
- Running into old friends who grew up your son/daughter
- People socially drinking or smoking
- A particular room in the house where your child passed away
- A certain sound that happened at the event
- Objects that were used in a child's death
- Sirens or other types of sounds that were there when it happened
- A particular smell that was present at the time it happened
- Pregnant women or women with small babies
- Weddings, funerals and other events

The goal in this session is to help you learn to identify if you have any triggers or corresponding plan that anticipates and deescalates the power of the trigger. We will be covering some healthy coping strategies to help you through these areas.

If you have some strong triggers that are impacting your life, we would highly recommend that you seek out professional counseling to help you learn skills to calm your brain's emotional responses to these triggers.

Many Grieving Moms may also be experiencing trauma known as Post Traumatic Stress Disorder (PTSD).

---

2 https://psychcentral.com/lib/what-is-a-trigger/

Trigger Events and Coping Skills

Post-Traumatic Stress Disorder
1. *Re-experiencing the trauma*—Flashbacks, nightmares, intrusive thoughts, etc.
2. *Avoidance*—Trying to avoid thoughts, feelings, situations, or people who might remind you of the trauma
3. *Hyperarousal*—Always being on alert, trouble sleeping, irritability, difficulty concentrating, exaggerated startle response

Some other associated symptoms of PTSD are: panic attacks, chronic pain, feeling of mistrust, substance abuse, relationship problems or suicidal thoughts.

You may also have forgetfulness and irrational thinking at times. Don't be too alarmed if you can't remember where you parked your car!

Quick Share

Share with the group some of the triggers or symptoms you are experiencing.

> **This next part, "What we think on" is very important, so make sure you cover this with your group. The goal is to have the women no longer dwell on the day their child died and rehearse it over and over in their mind, but to replace those thoughts with Scripture and positive thoughts God has given them over the situation.**

WHAT WE THINK ON

Many times, moms will repeat the event associated with the passing of their child over and over again in their head. Whether the memory was of being present when the child passed, coming onto the scene with police and sirens, or being in a totally different city or country, there are specific memories associated with that event.

Guilt and shame can become part of this unhealthy exercise as it's repeated over and over as a Trigger Event. The would of, could of, and should of creep in and keep us stuck. We have a choice to either dwell on that day when the Landslide hit and stay in the Frozen Phase, or we can remember the years of life we did have with our child by choosing to dwell on the good memories and the happy times with our child.

This may be something we need to do every five minutes at the beginning, but if we continually practice thinking about the good things about our child and not the day of the Landslide, then it will help us to move forward and continue our journey of healing.

> *We demolish arguments and every pretension that sets itself up against the knowledge of God, and we take captive every thought to make it obedient to Christ.* 2 Corinthians 10:5

Trigger Events and Coping Skills

ARREST YOUR ANXIETY

Triggers can cause anxiety, fear, or panic. Anxiety reminds me of climbing up the side of a very icy mountain that appears insurmountable and because of its mysteriousness and intimidation we lose confidence with every step. Suddenly, we start sliding down and spinning head over heels and we can't stop!

In mountaineering, the ice axe is a tool used to arrest the unexpected fall using a special technique done by planting the pick of the axe into the icy snow.

Here is a technique to arrest the anxiety that you're experiencing facing this mountain that seems insurmountable and to help you from sliding down out of control.

Quick Activity

1. Stop wherever you are.
2. Breathe slowly in your nose and out of your mouth. You will notice your breathing becomes shallow and intermittent or you may need to slow it down.
3. Begin by tensing up the muscles in your face…breathe…relax them
4. Tighten your neck muscles…breathe…relax them
5. Tighten your shoulder muscles…breathe…relax them
6. Tighten your gluteal muscles…breathe…relax them
7. Tighten your leg muscles…breathe…relax them
8. Tighten and curl your toes…breathe…relax them
9. Repeat if necessary

Let's try this together right now. Do #1-#9 as a group.

Trigger Events and Coping Skills

COPING SKILLS

UNHEALTHY COPING SKILLS

Many moms turn to unhealthy ways of coping through the sheer pain and grief of losing a child. Here are some very common unhealthy ways to cope during the grief.

- *Drinking*
  Many moms will turn to drinking to numb the pain of their grief. It is very common for the normal one or two glasses of wine each night to turn into a whole bottle.

- *Self-medicated Drugs*
  Doctors may have prescribed drugs to help you sleep or other type medication. These prescriptions may be good at first, but be aware that they can be habit forming. We want to maintain our good habits and not acquire new dependencies that will be harmful in the future.

- *Eating*
  There is a reason they call it 'comfort food'. Food does affect our brain and brings us a temporary comfort, but the side effects of weight gain, lethargy, and general ill feelings do not benefit us overall. It has been proven eating foods that raise your blood sugar levels (i.e. processed or sugary food) raise a person's risk for developing depression. Diets higher in fruits and vegetables are associated with lower risk of depression.

  Sometimes instead of eating too much, we may abstain from food all together because we experience a loss of appetite and enjoyment for our favorite foods. We can become too tired or too emotional to eat. Either extreme is not the goal.

- *Excessive Exercising*
  Some moms turn to excessive exercise. Exercise gives us a euphoric high in the form of endorphins. Too much exercise without consulting a medical professional first could cause harm to your joints, muscles, and organs.

- *Infidelity*
  Sex is a very strong form of euphoric and physical pleasure that can temporarily cover over our grief, numbing us from what has happened. Intimacy is very important in a marriage to keep couples strong and closely knitted. However, many men may turn to infidelity during this grieving time, and women are also susceptible to an affair as well. There may be a time after the loss of a child when a couple may not be intimate for a while and this is normal, but gradually coming back into a physical relationship with your husband will bring you closer together.

Trigger Events and Coping Skills

SUMMARY

Each of these unhealthy coping skills can be a substitute or replacement for God's true comfort that He wants to give us. God has sent his Holy Spirit and He is called the 'comforter'. When we substitute these comforts instead of allowing God to comfort us, then it results in addictive behaviors that replace the healthy ones that God desires for us.

> *If you love me...I will ask the Father and he will give you another Comforter, and he will never leave you. He is the Holy Spirit, the Spirit who leads into all truth. The world at large cannot receive him, for it isn't looking for him and doesn't recognize him. But you do, for he lives with you now and someday shall be in you.* John 14:16-17

Quick Share

Share with the group any unhealthy ways you have coped in your grieving.
Reminder: This is a confidential group and everything that is shared stays in the group.

> **Make sure to stress that this is a confidential and safe group in which to share.**

Spindrift Thoughts

"Just one more glass of wine...it won't hurt anything, and I'll be able to sleep better."
> *Don't drink too much wine. That cheapens your life. Drink the Spirit of God, huge draughts of him. Sing hymns instead of drinking songs! Sing songs from your heart to Christ. Sing praises over everything, any excuse for a song to God the Father in the name of our Master, Jesus Christ.* Ephesians 5:18-20 (MSG)

"I can keep eating to make me feel better. I can't stop myself anyways!"
> *Peace I leave with you; my peace I give to you. Not as the world gives do I give to you. Let not your hearts be troubled, neither let them be afraid.* John 14:27a

> *Do not join those who drink too much wine or gorge themselves on meat, for drunkards and gluttons become poor, and drowsiness clothes them in rags.* Proverbs 23:20-21

"It's just not fair that I have to go through this!"

Trigger Events and Coping Skills

The world is unprincipled. It's dog-eat-dog out there! The world doesn't fight fair. But we don't live or fight our battles that way—never have and never will. 2 Corinthians 10:3-4 (MSG)

HEALTHY COPING SKILLS

- **Healthy Eating**

  Eating is essential to how we feel, even on a good day. We need that fuel to combat our bodies huge stress and grieving levels, as well as for strength in being around a lot of people that come in and out of our home at this time. Eating healthy is essential to helping us heal and recover in our grief.

- **Good Sleep**

  Sleepless nights, tossing and turning with worry, fear and anxiety is not good during our time of grief and recover. Carefully selected audiobooks and worship music to meditate on is helpful to quiet our bodies and minds. Choosing not to eat or drink too many liquids, especially caffeinated beverages before bed, is also important.

- **Avoid Making Major Decisions**

  During this grieving time, it is tempting to do some major things in an attempt to not 'feel' the pain we are experiencing. Some examples are: selling your house, moving out of state, getting a divorce, buying unnecessary material things, changing jobs, getting a pet, or adopting a child.

- **New Beginnings**

  Things will never be the same as they used to be when your child was still with you. For some, the sheer stress of watching their child struggle with using drugs or other self-destructive behaviors is gone, but now replaced by the grief of their loss. While other moms may not have seen it coming, losing their child in an instant, some moms may have only carried their child in their womb for a brief amount of time before their loss. Whatever the case, life will never be the same as it was before. Give yourself the time and grace to adjust to this new way of living. For most, it will take a long time to fall into a normal rhythm again. Things won't be the same—just different.

Trigger Events and Coping Skills

Activity

What are some ways that you have coped with your grief in a healthy way?
What are some activities that you can do as a group to bring you closer and help you heal?

GROUP IDEA

One of the groups began walking and hiking together to get exercise and spend some time together.

Moving Forward

- Write down some ways that you have coped that are not healthy.
- Write some corresponding Scriptures to help you with healthy coping skills.
- Ask the Holy Spirit to comfort you when you are tempted to cope in an unhealthy way this week.

Closing Prayer

Preview of Next Week

Family Dynamics
Next week we will be discussing how other members of the family grieve differently.

Moving Forward Journal

Write down some ways that you have coped that are not healthy.

_____
_____
_____
_____
_____
_____
_____
_____
_____
_____
_____
_____

Write down some Scripture verses that have helped you.

_____
_____
_____
_____
_____
_____
_____
_____
_____
_____
_____
_____
_____

Prayer Requests

Name:_____
Situation: _____
_____
_____
_____

Name:_____
Situation: _____
_____
_____
_____

Name:_____
Situation: _____
_____
_____
_____

Name:_____
Situation: _____
_____
_____
_____

Name:_____
Situation: _____
_____
_____
_____

SESSION SIX

*"Families are not awesome by accident,
you have to fight for your family."*
Pastor Rick Warren

OPENING PRAYER

KEY SCRIPTURE

Families love through all kinds of weather, and families stick together in all kinds of trouble. Proverbs 17:17 (MSG)

SHARING

Last week we talk about triggers and coping skills.
Was there anything you learned that you implemented this week?

VIDEO

Coming soon.

DISCUSSION

We will be discussing the different ways in which family members deal with their grief.

Each woman will be in a different place in their lives, so we have covered both the single moms and the married women in this session, along with siblings. This session is longer and has a lot of material, so feel free to choose what is appropriate to your group. For example, if there are no single moms in the group then you can skip that section, etc.

Family Dynamics

DISCUSSION

Mourning involves the whole family and not only the individual. Ideally, the entire family can be involved in the healing process, but every member of the family is different in the way they will express their sorrow, now or in the future.

Some families have tightly held beliefs on how and when they are 'allowed' to show grief. These beliefs or rules can be spoken or unspoken. Some of the messages range from "It is okay to cry all the time" to "Suck it up and be strong" and every message in between. Depending on the messages, they can either help or prevent family members from truly grieving.

FAMILIES DEAL WITH GRIEF DIFFERENTLY

Each family member mourns in their own unique way. Some members of the family may want to talk about the child that died, while others may wince every time the name of that child is brought up. We can't force our way of expression of sorrow onto them and neither can they force their way onto us. Ultimately, don't put yourself or others in a box of what is "expected."

Feel the feelings you feel.

If you want to cry, then cry; if you want to laugh about a funny memory about your child or a situation that just happened, it's ok to laugh. Let your heart rest in knowing that the mourning process is very natural. Allowing yourself to feel the feelings you have will bring healing. Tears and laughter, although seen as opposing feelings, are available for our healing.

DIFFERENCES IN GRIEVING

As a mom losing a child, it can be devastating to pick up the pieces and continue on 'like normal' with the rest of the family. Your responsibilities and sense of order in the home is challenging to keep up with while you are still grieving.

Men may have a different way of grieving then women. Women tend to communicate, wanting to share their emotions, feeling a sense of responsibility for every member of family while they are grieving. Men tend to withdraw to their work, hobbies, or physical activities, and may not want to talk about how they are feeling. As wives, we may get easily offended by this behavior, feeling as if they don't care, but we need to keep in mind they are dealing with the grief in a completely different way. Physical intimacy may increase or it may decrease depending on the man.

Each person is very unique and different in their grieving, but here are some general ways that men and women differ in their grieving.

Family Dynamics

> These next sessions are broad generalizations about each gender and the siblings. Keep in mind that their own situations may be a bit different and the women can share about their own particular situations.

A WOMAN'S GRIEF

Women tend to grieve more deeply in an intense manner and for longer periods of time. As a mom we gave birth to our child and have a very deep connection from the moment they were in our womb to the day they were born. Or maybe we have miscarried a child in our womb.

As moms, we are busy in the daily activities surrounding us in motherhood. From changing diapers to carpooling to watching them now drive—we have been there in our child's life through it all. We are closely attached in all these ways that, after our child is gone, we see daily reminders of them. Their favorite box of cereal in the cabinet or the favorite sweater they wore—are all reminders of them on a daily basis

COMMON NEEDS OF WOMEN
- Relate face to face
- Most are external processors—are more expressive of their feelings to others
- Want to communicate their feelings and talk
- Like to be held
- Cry on their husband's or friend's shoulder
  This is not considered weak, but healthy
- Tend to grieve longer

Some common things, we, as a wife, may want from our husbands during the grieving time is to communicate our feelings, to be held and comforted, or cry on his shoulder. But many times, we may find our husband unavailable or checked out. We may be tempted to be offended and withdraw both physically and emotionally, which is not always healthy for our marriage. The grief makes us feel numb especially towards any type of physical intimacy with our husbands. We feel like we can never again feel joy and happiness while our child is gone and that somehow that diminishes their memory. If there was a miscarriage, then fear of pregnancy may result. Single moms may try to find solace in their friends, only to find their friends don't know how to handle this death and become distant.

You don't have to grieve forever to prove your love for you child or their memory.

Family Dynamics

A MAN'S GRIEF

Men don't always grieve the same as women, even when it is the same loss of a child. Men like to 'fix it'. If you have a problem, then many times they assume you want the answer to fix the situation, when all you may want is for them to just listen and for you to be heard. Men are more action driven and focus more on tasks than on relationships. They define who they by their work rather than their emotional ties. Because of this action-driven focus, their grief becomes far more inward and less expressive. Suck it up–toughen up–don't show your emotions are common mores of our society. Real men don't cry and it is a sign of weakness. They are tough and in control. Real men know what to do in a crisis, and they are strong enough to support the rest of the family. Because of this and the fact that a man doesn't grieve the same way as a woman, it may make it tougher for men to go through the grieving process.

COMMON NEEDS OF MEN

- Relate side-by-side
- Communication while doing some type of activity
- Most are internal processors–cry alone or in secret
- Want physical activities or work
- May seem more aloof when dealing with grief
- Don't want to do anything that seems 'weak' in our culture
  They have to be perceived as strong for their family
- Desire physical intimacy as a way to connect
- May not grieve as long as a woman
- May perceive his wife as over-reacting by crying so much while he has to hold it together

Some common things a man may want during the grieving time is some discretion so that they can deal with their emotions in private. They may seem more aloof, yet at the same time want physical intimacy as a way to connect to their wife, find comfort, and escape the grief. Some men, however lose interest in sex, because they feel like they have failed the family and couldn't protect their child. Feelings of worthlessness and inadequacy hinder them from being sexually intimate with their wife. Reaffirming them and your continual respect for them will help assure them that they didn't fail.

There are many ways that men grieve that do not involve tears. This can be misconstrued as not caring. Just like a mom can blame herself for seemingly not being there for her child, a husband as a provider and protector can feel a sense of failure, too. Shame and helplessness are common feelings they deal with, convinced they somehow failed the family by not preventing their child's death.

Family Dynamics

A COUPLE'S GRIEF

Each parent related and was emotionally connected to their child in a different and unique way. Their own personal identity, as well as their identity as a couple, has been hugely impacted. The marriage itself looks different now. They will need to redefine what it will be like to be in a marriage again without their child. Part of their legacy is now gone. If the child who passed away was their only child, then the parents have a huge sense of loss of legacy and posterity, which is now completely gone. Depending on what happened to the child, parents can also feel remorse or guilt for not protecting their child or for not 'seeing it coming.'

Couples—remember to be there for one another. It is okay to grieve on your own, but don't shut each other out. Set aside some time to listen, to talk, to do things together, and to love on each other. Let love be the motivation for everything you do.

COMMON NEEDS FOR COUPLES
- Grieve separately or together
- May not be emotionally available to the other spouse
- Partner can't meet all of our needs
- Seek support from wide range of people
- Rebuild life at partner's pace (may be slower than yours)
- Don't make any major decisions as a couple for a year

Quick Share

Share how your grieving has been different from your spouse or other men in your life.

Family Dynamics

A SINGLE MOM'S GRIEF

Being a single mom is hard in normal circumstances, let alone if you have lost a child. It can be devastating and the isolation can be even more debilitating as a single mom. God's Word speaks to this specifically. Single moms in our society are similar to the widows of the Bible. God spoke many times about the widows and how he would take care of them.

COMMON NEEDS FOR SINGLE MOMS
- Ask God to show you—you're not alone
- Ask God to bring friends into your children's life to comfort them, too
- Have open and honest communication about their sibling's passing
- Be consistent and available to your other children
- Check in often to see how your other children are doing
- If you don't have any other children, then know that God is with you
  You're not alone!

A SIBLING'S GRIEF

Children and siblings don't grieve the same as adults. Children may process their grief differently at different developmental stages. Their feelings of grief can come and go throughout the years. It may hit them later in life.

If they are younger children, they do not yet fully understand the finality of death. Ask questions to find out how much they really know about death. Then give them age-appropriate answers.

If they are older children, then they may experience grief and it may reappear later on in subsequent years. The teenage years are tumultuous as it is, let alone adding the death of a sibling into that time frame. They may be very conflicted, wanting to be okay around their peers, then breaking down at other times.

Some siblings may have unfounded fears that you will die or leave them, too. Reassure them that you will not leave them and that you will be there for them. Grief will be a new feeling for them and they may not know how to process it. Give them attention and time to talk to you about how they feel. If they are younger, you can have them draw or color on a piece of paper what they are feeling, and then talk about the picture with you.

Family Dynamics

COMMON NEEDS OF SIBLINGS
- Need to know that they are safe and that things will be okay
- Giving them physical affection, such as a hug, will go a long way towards them feeling safe
- Validate what they are thinking and encourage them to share their feelings
- Give them permission to grieve
- Reassure them you will not leave them
- You don't have to shield them from grief
- Be open and honest in communication

Don't feel like you have to shield your children from the grief. In our society, we don't want our children to experience pain, and yet they will need to go through the grieving process just as much as you do. Be open and honest in your communication with them.

Avoid some of the common responses to death such as, God took your brother/sister to Heaven because they were his special angel. Comments like this may instill fear that God is going to take them next! Another common response from others your child may encounter is, "Just be strong for your mom and dad." Have an open and honest conversation about how they don't have to be strong for you and that by grieving, they are being strong.

If they are older children, suicidal thoughts may prevail in their minds thinking that they can see their sibling again sooner rather than later. Prayer is the best antidote to these types of thoughts. Continue in prayer over your child and have open and honest dialog about it as well.

Let them know it is okay to have joy again in their life and that it is not disloyal to their sibling's memory to be happy again.

As moms, make sure that we don't forget the children that are still alive, because of our deep grief over the child that has passed away. Those young children or adult children need you just as much as they ever have when someone dies.

Share something that stood out to you as a single mom, or helping your other children grieve.

Family Dynamics

Spindrift Thoughts

"The divorce rate is very high for couples who lose a child. Am I going to lose my marriage, because my child has died?"
Research by The Compassionate Friends reveals that the divorce rate for couples when a child has died is only 9%!

As a matter of fact, according to respected grief expert and noted author Harold Ivan Smith, research indicates that only 6% of marriages fail following the death of a child; the myth is 75% or higher. Dr. Smith went on to encourage those of us in the field of grief and bereavement counseling to do all we can to help debunk this myth.

"My husband is not there for me. I can't even cry on his shoulder!"
As mentioned, men like to fix it for us, that is their nature. Communicate exactly what you're needing. "I know you don't like to see me hurting, all I need is just to be held right now."

"My other children seem just fine, how did they get over it so fast?!"
Don't be alarmed if your other child is seemingly fine. It doesn't mean they don't care or are "over it." It could be a beautiful peace that God has given; the kind of peace the "passes all understanding." Be thankful for this blessing.

Conversely, it could be that your child has an outlet with their friends or a church support group that you are not a part of that has allowed them to express their feelings.

This may give the allusion that they are not mourning because they seem fine when they see you. Again, don't be alarmed or offended. It would be more offensive and hurtful if you asked them why they seem to be fine.

As an alternative, check in with your children, allow them the opportunity to talk and express their feelings with you, but don't be offended if they don't. Allow God to use others as a support, and pray that He shows you how you can best support your child through this.

FAMILY GRIEF

Whenever major life stresses hit, like a death in the family, it can either draw a family closer together or drive them further apart. Be intentional to bring the family closer together during this time.

Family Dynamics

When we are climbing up and out of our Landslide, we each have different emotional and physical strengths and limitations. If you're further ahead on your path, they won't hear you yelling back to them in the density of the woods. All you can do is look back and keep them in view so they are not getting lost and bewildered.

Get professional counseling with your entire family through this process. A professional can help you in specific areas that your family may be struggling with in the grieving process.

◎ Activity

What are some ways that God has met your needs in the past?
What are some needs that you currently have?

> **If a woman has a need that the group can help her with, then have the group rally together to help meet that particular need. (Matthew 5:42)**

◎ Moving Forward

We each have unique needs. People want to help you through your grieving, but they are unsure how to do that or what you need. This week you will be getting a 'voice' to ask for what you need. Many times as women we are always caring for others, but this week we are going to ask for what we need.

◎ Closing Prayer

◎ Preview of Next Week

Forgiveness
Next week we will be talking about the importance of forgiveness in our lives.

> **Encourage the women to come next week. This next session is one of the most power sessions in the program.**

Moving Forward Journal

It is easy to judge one another by the way we are grieving, but we each have unique needs. People want to help, but they may not know what to do to help you or what you need.

Get together with your family, surviving children, or friends and tell them what you need. They can't read your mind. Make sure to tell them you want them to listen and that they don't have to fix things, but that this is what you need.

Ask them to answer the same questions so that you can help each other through your mourning.

Use these statements to help you through this process.

1. When I cry, I need you to _____
2. When you want physical affection, I feel _____
3. When you cry, I feel _____
4. What I need most is _____
5. What do you need most? _____

What happened when you told someone what you needed?

_____
_____
_____
_____
_____
_____
_____
_____
_____
_____
_____

Prayer Requests

Name:_____

Situation: _____

_____

_____

_____

Name:_____

Situation: _____

_____

_____

_____

Name:_____

Situation: _____

_____

_____

_____

Name:_____

Situation: _____

_____

_____

_____

Name:_____

Situation: _____

_____

_____

_____

SESSION SEVEN

"Unforgiveness is a like a lodged pebble in your boot that penetrates deeper with every step."
Jacke Van Woerkom

This is very important session, and a breakthrough time for many of the Grieving Moms. Stay especially open to God this week as you walk through this session with the women.

OPENING PRAYER

KEY SCRIPTURE

Bear with each other and forgive one another if any of you has a grievance against someone. Forgive as the Lord forgave you. Colossians 3:13

SHARING

In the *Family Dynamics* session we discussed statements you could share with your loved ones.
Share how that helped you to move forward this week.

VIDEO

Coming soon.

DISCUSSION

We will be discussing how forgiveness is a huge part of our healing process and how to find freedom through forgiveness.

DISCUSSION

What do you do when you have stood on God's promises for your child's deliverance and then they died? Or you stood for their physical healing, even declaring God's Scriptures over them, and the healing did not happen? Or maybe you were completely caught off guard by an accident or a miscarriage.

Whatever the situation surrounding your child's passing, it is none the less devastating, whether we watched it happen slowly or suddenly, whether we had been rehearsing their funeral in our mind a thousand times because they were an addict, or whether it came suddenly.

Whatever the circumstances, our faith has been assaulted. How in the world did God allow this to happen? He is big and powerful. We go to church and the pastor says, 'just believe' and 'have faith'. But what do you do when it doesn't work out the way you thought it would?

These thoughts can cause regret and hurt, which in turn lead to offenses with God and others, and unforgiveness begins to fester inside of us.

Many of us have questions running through our minds.

> **Usually they start with the *If Onlys*:**
>
> "*If only* I had gotten him medical treatment earlier."
>
> "*If only* I had not divorced her dad."
>
> "*If only* I had taken him to a recovery center earlier."
>
> "*If only* I had taken care of my body better, I wouldn't have miscarried."
>
> "*If only* I had noticed some of the signs of depression."
>
> And on and on it goes...

The *if only* questions are useless regrets that keep us stuck in grief. We want to make sense of something that absolutely doesn't make sense.

> **As moms we want to know why:**
>
> "Why did this happen?"
>
> "Why did God allow this...couldn't He have stopped it?
>
> "He's big enough to have stopped it!"
>
> "Why couldn't I have stopped it?"
>
> "Why my child?"

Circle some of the thoughts above that have been running through your mind.

What's Next?

Rick Warren, Pastor of Saddleback church, has said that knowing your why, may end up actually hurting you more in the long run, so instead focus on the question, What's next?

> **Some of the women may still need to work through the above section, before they can go to the "What's Next?" question. This may take some time of healing before some of the women are ready to ask this question, but you can introduce this concept so that they know about it.**

You may not be ready to ask that question yet, but when you are, it is a powerful question to ask. You don't want to jump to that question until you have gone through the acute grieving period—you just won't be ready for that question.

However, when you are ready it is a very powerful question to ask. God never promises that we will not have trouble, what he does promise is that He will turn it around and use it for good.

> *We know that in all things God works for the good of those who love him, who have been called according to his purpose.* Romans 8:28

What good can God use from this huge hole in my heart?
Time will tell when and how God will use it and turn it around for our good.

"Why didn't God stop this—isn't he a good God?"
   The LORD is good to all; he has compassion on all he has made. Psalm 145:9

"If only I would have taken care of my body, I wouldn't have lost the baby."
   We don't always know the why, but we do know that God will work it into good in the end.
   He knows us far better than we know ourselves, knows our pregnant condition, and keeps us present before God. That's why we can be so sure that every detail in our lives of love for God is worked into something good. Romans 8:27-28 (MSG)

"Why wasn't my husband there for me when I needed him the most?"
Regardless of the why, God wants us to still forgive.
   Be gentle with one another, sensitive. Forgive one another as quickly and thoroughly as God in Christ forgave you. Ephesians 4:32b (MSG)

Caution Crevasse Ahead

In mountaineering, a crevasse is a deep open crack often seen when walking on a glacier. If you survive the fall, you won't last long due to the frigid temperatures and lack of its nurturing hospitality with little hope of being found!

Everyone's story regarding their circumstances revolving around the passing of their child is unique. Some moms may have been there while their child passed, while other moms may have showed up to ambulances and sirens. Yet other moms may have been in a completely different city or country. Whatever the case, those first images are forever etched into our memories.

As the memory of that day gets repeated over and over it gets deeper and deeper in our mind and spirit like being stuck in that crevasse—somehow thinking that if we keep replaying it there will be a different outcome.

Forgiveness is the first step towards moving forward from the bad memories; forgiving God, ourselves, and others. If we are willing to let go and forgive (even ourselves) we begin to heal and move forward. We first need to know some of the hidden things we are believing and allow God to show them to us.

Activity

In a quiet and prayerful environment, ask God the following questions and write down the impression you get. Write the first thing that comes into your mind.

What lie have I believed regarding my child's death?
_____
_____
_____
_____

What is your truth, God?
_____
_____
_____
_____

Share with the group your answers.

Forgiveness

Many of these Spindrift Thoughts revolve around people letting you down, and possibly feeling like God did, too. We may have grown up in a church where we never had the freedom to come to God with our complaints. God is big enough to handle not only our complaints, but our anger, too. Blaming is part of what we go through and blaming ourselves is very damaging.

Forgiveness is the key to moving forward.

Who to forgive?

Forgiveness is the key to moving forward. Forgiveness is a choice of the will, not a feeling of the heart. Choose to forgive, even if means you need to do it more than once a day, until your feelings catch up to your will.

Who should I forgive?
- God
- Spouse
- Your child
- Others
- Yourself

GOD – What are we holding against God in this situation?

BIBLICAL FACTS ABOUT GOD

☆ ***God is good all the time***
   You are good and do only good; make me follow your lead. Psalm 119:68 (TLB)

☆ ***God doesn't cause bad things to happen to teach us a lesson***
   For I know the plans I have for you…plans for welfare and not for evil, to give you a future and a hope. Jeremiah 29:11 (ESV)

☆ ***He gives everyone a free will that impacts themselves and the world around them***
   You…were called to be free. But do not use your freedom to indulge the flesh. Galatians 5:13a

☆ ***God promises to turn everything around in our favor***
   He knows us far better than we know ourselves…That's why we can be so sure that every detail in our lives…is worked into something good. Romans 8:28 (MSG)

Purpose in your heart to give up the why and focus on forgiving whatever you are holding against God in this situation. Purpose in your heart to continue to believe that God is good ALL the time, even if you don't understand why it happened.

SPOUSE – What are you holding against your spouse in this situation?

Maybe your spouse had a role to play in what happened to your child. Or maybe you really wanted them to be there for you and comfort you and they were unable.

YOUR CHILD – Did your child make poor choices in their life that led to their death?

Maybe they got involved with the wrong crowd, addictions, or life decisions. You may be angry that their decisions impacted your world or your grandchildren's lives in a harmful way.

OTHERS – Had someone else had a part to play in your child's death?

Maybe it was a perpetrator, a family member, or another that may have had a part to play in your child's death.

YOURSELF – What are you holding over yourself in terms of being responsible for what happened to your child?

Maybe you blame yourself because you were a single mom, working too much and not there for them, or allowed an abusive relationship to continue without seeking help and getting out. Maybe you feel like you 'should have known' or been there somehow.

Quick Share

In the list above, who is someone that you need to forgive?
It can be more than one person.

Forgiveness is a choice, not a feeling.
Are you ready to make the choice to forgive?

> **Encourage every woman to do this week's Moving Forward exercise. It will be a breakthrough activity for many of the moms. We would love to hear the stories of breakthrough. Feel free to email us at *info@grievingmoms.com* and share your stories.**

Forgiveness

◉ Moving Forward

Write a prayer letter of forgiveness to God. Include specific things you are choosing to forgive God or other people for. Remember to forgive is a choice, not a feeling.

State what you need to forgive and then write a prayer letter below of forgiveness. If you need more space than the journal space provided, feel free to write more on another sheet of paper.

> *For godly grief produces a repentance that leads to salvation without regret.*
> 2 Corinthians 7:10a (ESV)

Forgiving someone does not mean that you do not have boundaries with someone that is unhealthy or is abusive. You can forgive, but still have safe and proper boundaries with that person.

SPECIAL NOTE
This week it is very important that you do the Moving Forward activity and bring it with you to the group next week to share.

◉ Closing Prayer

◉ Preview of Next Week

Letting Go of our Child's Belongings
Next week we will talk about how we can let go of our child's belongings and how to save those items that are special to us.

Moving Forward Journal

You can use this outline for your letter and repeat the format for as many people that you need to forgive.

Dear God,

I choose to forgive _____(person/God) for _____
_____
_____
_____
_____
_____
_____

I have been holding this over you _____
_____
_____
_____
_____
_____
_____

Today I choose to let this offense go and _____
_____
_____
_____
_____
_____
_____

(You may use a separate piece of paper and follow this outline above for each person you need to forgive.)

If you have already forgiven people surrounding your Landslide, spend some quiet time with God and ask Him if there is anyone in your life you need to forgive. Wait quietly and see if anyone comes floating into your mind. Then use the outline above to forgive them.

Prayer Requests

Name:_____

Situation: _____

_____

_____

_____

Name:_____

Situation: _____

_____

_____

_____

Name:_____

Situation: _____

_____

_____

_____

Name:_____

Situation: _____

_____

_____

_____

Name:_____

Situation: _____

_____

_____

_____

Letting Go of our Child's Belongings

SESSION EIGHT

"When you can—you will."
Kay Warren

OPENING PRAYER

KEY SCRIPTURE

I prayed for this child, and the Lord has granted me what I asked of him. So now I give him to the Lord. For his whole life he will be given over to the Lord.
I Samuel 1:27-28a

SHARING

Share your forgiveness letters with the group.
This may be out of your comfort zone, but you will feel a huge release when you do this.

We would love to hear the stories of breakthrough. Feel free to email us at *info@grievingmoms.com* and share your stories.

VIDEO

Coming soon.

DISCUSSION

We will be discussing ways to let go of some of our child's belongings and which items to keep.

Letting Go of our Child's Belongings

DISCUSSION

One of the biggest decisions we have as Grieving Moms is when and how we let go of our child's physical items in the house or in their house if they were adults.

Letting go is both an emotional state and a physical one, too. As we have gone through some of the phases of the grieving process, we have learned to begin to accept the Landslide that has come. Everyone lets go of their children's belongings in different ways and we need to honor the way each person does this.

Some people may want to take everything out of their room and box it up right away so that they don't look at it every day. While others, slowly box up things over time. Some moms may even keep the room exactly like it is—a museum of memories of their child. If you are living with someone who wants to box everything up right away and you do not, it can be challenging and you may feel additional hurt and pain over the situation. Conversely, if the other person wants everything to remain around the home and you do not want the constant reminder of what happened, that can be just as challenging as well.

Your adult child may have been married, adding a whole new layer in deciding what to do with their belongings. It may be a daughter-in-law that just decides to throw out all the belongings. She lost a husband, but you lost a child…very different.

Conversations to reconcile this delicate subject are necessary, but may be very difficult. To have peace between family members it is best to drop defenses before beginning. Asking where each of you are in your journey is important.

You may want to start with:
> *"I know this isn't an easy thing to talk about, but can we come to a respectful agreement with regards to some of my child's personal items?"*

TIPS FOR TALKING TO FAMILY MEMBERS

- Open communication with the family
- Ask the other person how they feel about your child's belongings
- Find out which items are important to each family member
- Tell the other family members how you feel about boxing up your child's stuff
- Compromise about what to display and what to box up
- Find ways to transform some of their belongings into one memorable keepsake
- Don't take anything without the other family members knowing

Letting Go of our Child's Belongings

Why We Hold On

We want to remember our child through their items they've collected over the years. Each time we see those items, we remember our child in a special way or smell their scent on their clothing to bring back their memory. Their items represent them and remind us of our relationship with them. Some may carry good memories, but some may not have good memories, depending on the circumstances.

Letting Go of Your Child's Belongings

You will know when the time is right to begin letting your child's possessions go when you have peace about it and not dread and fear. When it is time to let go of things they possessed, it is important to have a friend come with you to sort out what you will keep, give away, or discard. Letting go of their things is one of the most stressful experiences in this grieving time. It may take months before you are emotionally ready to tackle this project. For some, this may be easier to do than for others.

In the Grieving Moms support group, this is a 'No Judgement Zone', so however long it takes is okay as long as you are moving forward in your process of healing. Some items will have more sentimental value than others and bring back a host of memories. You may open up a box at Christmas time and then suddenly curl up on the floor in tears because the memories come flooding back.

Tackle this project in steps and as you are emotionally ready to let go. Do not feel guilty if you donate or discard some of their things. Come up with a timeframe to finish this project. You don't want to hurry to avoid the process, but you don't want to be too rushed either. There have been moms who have let go of their child's belongings in haste and then regretted not hanging onto some of their precious things.

Plan blocks of time to work on this with a close friend or family member. There is no right or wrong time – just 'let time have time'. Listen to your heart, and if you don't want to go through their things yet, then don't. You can wait until you have a peace about it and you'll know when it is the right time.

Tips for Letting Go:
- Take your time
- Have a trusted friend help you
- Come up with a timeframe if that helps you move forward
- Plan blocks of time
- Listen to your heart

Letting Go of our Child's Belongings

Quick Share

Share some ways you have let go of your child's belongings.
Do you still have items that are hard to let go?

> Tell the women that, in a couple of weeks, they can bring their remembrance items to share with the group.

Spindrift Thoughts

"If I let go of my child's things, then I won't have a way to remember them anymore."
> Jesus said to her, "I am the resurrection and the life. Whoever believes in me, though he die, yet shall he live, and everyone who lives and believes in me shall never die. Do you believe this?"
> John 11:25-26 (ESV)

"I'm afraid of letting go because I feel that I will be letting go of their memories."
> Fear not, for I am with you; be not dismayed, for I am your God; I will strengthen you, I will help you, I will uphold you with my righteous right hand. Isaiah 41:10 (ESV)

> He will wipe away every tear from their eyes, and death shall be no more, neither shall there be mourning, nor crying, nor pain anymore, for the former things have passed away.
> Revelation 21:4 (ESV)

"Does God really know what it is like to lose a child?"
> This is how much God loved the world: He gave his Son, his one and only Son. And this is why: so that no one need be destroyed; by believing in him, anyone can have a whole and lasting life. God didn't go to all the trouble of sending his Son merely to point an accusing finger, telling the world how bad it was. He came to help, to put the world right again. John 3:16-17 (MSG)

God is the God of all comfort. He knows exactly what you have gone through. It is a huge comfort to know that God is a 'Grieving Father'. He not only lost his son to death, but freely gave Jesus to us because of his great love towards us.

Letting Go of our Child's Belongings

"Will I be able to preserve and protect the memory of my child?"

End? No, the journey doesn't end here. Death is just another path. One that we all must take.
J.R.R. Tolkien - The Return of the King

Quick Share

Share any of these Spindrift Thoughts that you have experienced.

REMEMBERANCE

Jesus cared enough to leave something for us to remember him. Jesus made a special Passover in the upper room and His disciples took communion to remember Him after He was gone. What a beautiful Savior to take the time to give us a way to remember Him after He was gone! Remembering people is important to God. It is important that we keep our child's memory alive. One way to do this is through their belongings. There are items that you will want to keep as a remembrance of your child and to honor their life.

KEEPING SOME OF THEIR BELONGINGS

It is important that we keep some of our child's belongings that are special to us. Many times, we can take some of their possessions and make a special item from it. One of the Grieving Moms in the GM Community took her son's pants and cut out all the pockets on them and then had a quilt made from them. She called it, "Pockets of Love."

Another Grieving Mom took a beautiful picture of her son, created many small patches from it and gave them out to hikers on the trail in Yosemite in remembrance of his favorite place.

Displaying Items

Some of the most treasured items can be displayed in a prominent place in the house, bringing your child to remembrance. You do not have to keep every single item they owned that is sentimental. You may want to give some of those types of items to other family members or close relatives or friends. If you do not have room to display an item, you can take a picture of it to save it so that you can continue to look at it for years to come. You can create a keepsake box and put those pictures and other sentimental things in the box. You can also make a memory bear or quilts from their clothing.

Letting Go of our Child's Belongings

IDEAS FOR THEIR BELONGINGS

- Quilts and pillows from their clothing
- Patch of their picture to put on backpacks and clothing
- T-Shirt pillows
- Child ashes etched into a tattoo
- Military flag displayed or dog tags
- Make shirts with favorite picture of your child

*** The GM website has some of these services that we provide to the GM Community ***
www.grievingmoms.com

On the GM website we have some ways that the women can take their children's clothing or belongings and turn them into memorial items. Have the women go to *www.grievingmoms.com/store* for more information on these memorial items.

Activity

Share some of the ways you have displayed your child's belongings.
In a couple of weeks, you will have an opportunity to bring those items to share with the GM group.

Moving Forward

Do something for YOU this week!

As a group, come up with some ideas of what the women can do this week for themselves.

Closing Prayer

Preview of Next Week

Dealing with Other People
We will be discussing ways in which you can handle difficult situations with people in your life.

Moving Forward Journal

Do something just for you this week!
- Make it memorable.
- Pick something that you really enjoy—something that you have not been able to do in a long time for yourself.

List some ideas for things that you can do for yourself this week and commit to doing at least one of them.

1. _____
2. _____
3. _____
4. _____
5. _____

If the timing is right, then begin to clean out one area of your child's room or their possessions.

Tell us about that experience this week.

_____
_____
_____
_____
_____
_____
_____
_____
_____
_____
_____
_____
_____
_____

Prayer Requests

Name:_____

Situation: _____

_____

_____

_____

Name:_____

Situation: _____

_____

_____

_____

Name:_____

Situation: _____

_____

_____

_____

Name:_____

Situation: _____

_____

_____

_____

Name:_____

Situation: _____

_____

_____

_____

Dealing with Other People

SESSION NINE

"They don't know—what they don't know."
Sharon Kotsonas,
Grieving Mom, AZ

OPENING PRAYER

KEY SCRIPTURE

Be kind to one another, tenderhearted, forgiving one another, as God in Christ forgave you. Ephesians 4:32 (ESV)

SHARING

Share some special thing that you did just for you last week.
Were you able to let go of any of your child's belongings?

VIDEO

Coming soon.

DISCUSSION

We will be discussing ways we can handle the hurtful things that others say to us.

Dealing with Other People

DISCUSSION

Job's Comforters

In the Bible, there is a story of a man named Job who lost ALL of his seven sons and three daughters in a single day, along with all of his possessions. What is recounted as well is that his wife was a Grieving Mom. His wife was the only one to survive, but all she could tell him was to 'curse God and die.' She was not much of a comfort but can you blame her? She had just lost ALL ten of her children. A mother's worst nightmare!

Job's friends sat Shiva with him and did not say anything for a long time, but when they did speak, it was not very encouraging. They blamed Job for everything that happened and told him that this was all his fault and that he must have sinned and that is why this happened.

We may have well-meaning friends who do not say the right things. Many times their words are downright hurtful. They can become selfish and make it all about themselves, or at the very least say something that is very insensitive.

- ✯ Have you experienced a friend who distances themselves from you because your situation is just too heavy for them?
- ✯ Did you have well-meaning friends say very hurtful things to you?

Many of the Grieving Moms feel 'alone, but not alone.' Not many people understand, nor do we expect them to, yet the sun rises and the sun sets every day around us and life happens in the midst of it.

At the end of Job's story, God asked him to forgive his friends for what they said. Only after he forgave them did God restore double everything that he lost materially, as well as giving him ten more children!

Forgiving those who say insensitive things, and knowing how to respond in the appropriate way is imperative for us in moving forward in the next chapter that God has for us.
God did not cause your child to die. But God's promise is that He will turn every situation around for your good.

> *Meanwhile, the moment we get tired in the waiting, God's Spirit is right alongside helping us along. If we don't know how or what to pray, it doesn't matter. He does our praying in and for us, making prayer out of our wordless sighs, our aching groans. He knows us far better than we know ourselves, knows our pregnant condition, and keeps us present before God. That's why we can be so sure that every detail in our lives of love for God is worked into something good.* Romans 8:28 (MSG)

Dealing with Other People

RESPONDING WITH GENTLE ANSWERS

The pain in our hearts is so deep, yet responding with a harsh answer may shut down those we truly care about. Instead, practice a gentler way to respond.

A gentle answer turns away wrath, but a harsh word stirs up anger. Proverbs 15:1

Here are some of the common questions or comments people may say to us:

How are you?
"Thank you for asking, just taking life a day at a time."

Time is a healer, it's been a few months, I bet you're starting to feel like yourself.
"Oh (insert name), I am forever changed since I lost my child. I am trusting God to restore my broken heart and fill me with a different joy."

Your child is just a little angel in Heaven smiling down on you.
"Yes, it is comforting to know she is in Heaven, but until I see her, I want to fulfill God's purpose here."

God only takes his best angels to Heaven first
"Honestly, with all due respect, that's not correct theology."

Call me if you need anything
"Most of the time it is best to call them. Many times your friends feel awkward talking to you and they just want to do something for you, but may not know what you need.

I'm sorry I haven't called or come over, I just don't know what to say and it is so hard for me.
"I understand it is hard for you, maybe we can just watch a movie together."

During this time, God may do a bit of friend sorting during these challenging circumstances. Don't take it personally. People are all very different and perhaps they've never experienced any pain or grief.

A despairing man should have the devotion of his friends. Job 6:14a

It is important to speak the truth in love to others.

Dealing with Other People

Here is an example of what you could say:
"I realize what has happened is tough for most to hear, but I know the family and friends that God has in our life were given the ability to walk with us through this sorrowful season."
"I bring no scales with me to the table as we are sharing prayer requests together as friends."

 ## Quick Share

What are some things that people have said to you?
How have you responded to these comments from family and friends?

> **These comments may have come recently or in the past.**

Sharon is a Grieving Mom in Arizona. One of things she said to herself when insensitive comments were made...
  "*They just don't know—what they don't know.*"

Most of your friends have not lost a child and have no idea what to say. Most of the time they are doing the best they can to say something that would cheer you up.

Have no expectations about who shows up in your life, who is there for you, and who is not. Don't be surprised if a close friend or some family members aren't the ones that show up to lavish you with love and lasagna!

 ## Spindrift Thoughts

"**I don't want to forgive others for the insensitive things they have said.**"
  Bearing with one another and, if one has a complaint against another, forgiving each other; as the Lord has forgiven you, so you also must forgive. Colossians 3:13 (ESV)

"**Have they tried putting themselves in my shoes?!**"

Dealing with Other People

Do not repay evil for evil or reviling for reviling, but on the contrary, bless, for to this you were called, that you may obtain a blessing. 1 Peter 3:9 (ESV)

"After all these years of being friends, now when I lose my child they walk away because they can't handle it?"

Jesus said, Father, forgive them, for they do not know what they are doing. And they divided up his clothes by casting lost. Luke 23:24

GOD IS FAMILIAR WITH GRIEF
John 11

Jesus' friend Lazarus was sick and his sister sent for Jesus to come and heal him. In this story of Lazarus, Jesus purposely waited many days before coming to him and by then, Lazarus had died. Jesus had every intention to raise him from the dead, yet have you ever noticed that famous Scripture that everyone memorizes? "Jesus wept."

Why did Jesus weep if He knew He was going to raise Lazarus from the dead within minutes? Jesus felt their grief and loss and had compassion on them.

Today we have a Heavenly Father who knows our grief and can relate in every way. Even when others do not know how to relate or what to say, we have a good God who has grieved and knows what we are going through.

Now that we know what we have—Jesus, this great High Priest with ready access to God—let's not let it slip through our fingers. We don't have a priest who is out of touch with our reality. He's been through weakness and testing, experienced it all—all but the sin. So let's walk right up to Him and get what He is so ready to give. Take the mercy, accept the help. Hebrews 4:14-16 (MSG)

TELL OTHERS WHAT YOU NEED

It is absolutely okay and very healthy to tell others what you need. You will have people in your life that really do want to help, but they have not experienced the passing of a child.

As moms, we are always concerned with what others think of us or we are busy taking care of others. This is a time when it is completely alright and necessary to take care of ourselves.

Dealing with Other People

"I need" statements are some of the toughest things to say when we are a mom, but it is very important that we verbally tell people what we need.

Use these statements with friends and family:
- I need you to do _____
- I like it when you _____
- I appreciate it when you _____
- It makes me feel better when _____
- That was so comforting when you said _____

When you can educate those around you on what you need and want, it will help them to be a better friend and it will help you, too!

> Encourage the women to do the Moving Forward activity this week.

Activity

Why is it so hard for us as moms to verbally tell someone what we need?
Do you have a 'supermom' mentality or a fear of rejection and not getting your needs met?

Moving Forward

Fill in the statements below:
- I need you to do _____
- I like it when you _____
- I appreciate it when you _____
- It makes me feel better when _____
- That was so comforting when you said _____

Come up with a list of gentle responses that you can use while interacting with friends, family, and those you may run into out in public.

Use one of these responses this week and talk about it in the group next week.

Closing Prayer

Preview of Next Week

Anniversaries, Birthdays, and Holidays
Next week we will be discussing these special days and how we can handle these difficult milestones.

Moving Forward Journal

Come up with a list of loving and gentler responses that you can use when interacting with friends, family, and those you may run into out in public.

Use these statements with friends and family:

- I need you to do _____
_____
_____

- I like it when you _____
_____
_____

- I appreciate it when you _____
_____
_____

- It makes me feel better when _____
_____
_____

- That was so comforting when you said_____
_____
_____

Prayer Requests

Name:_____
Situation: _____
_____
_____
_____

Name:_____
Situation: _____
_____
_____
_____

Name:_____
Situation: _____
_____
_____
_____

Name:_____
Situation: _____
_____
_____
_____

Name:_____
Situation: _____
_____
_____
_____

Anniversaries, Birthdays & Holidays

SESSION TEN

"Sometimes you will never know the true value of a moment until it becomes a memory."
Theodor Seuss Geisel

OPENING PRAYER

KEY SCRIPTURE
"When Jesus had given thanks, he broke it and said...do this in remembrance of me." 1 Corinthians 11:24

SHARING
Share how you felt when you told people what you needed last week.

VIDEO
Coming soon.

DISCUSSION
We will be discussing specials days of the year and tips to handling those times of the year.

Anniversaries, Birthdays & Holidays

DISCUSSION

Remembering our children

Many times, special occasions like anniversaries, birthdays, or holidays can be difficult for families who have lost a child. Days or even months leading up to an anniversary of your child's passing or special holiday can become very challenging emotionally. A lot of moms have found comfort in talking about their child and remembering them, especially on these critical days. It may have been an extremely tough road for you and your current memories of your child may not have been so wonderful due to addiction or other issues, however, if you go back to their childhood that may serve as a solace in your remembrance of them. For others, you have some amazing memories and it may be hard to create some new ones because you want to hold onto the old ones so tightly. Whatever your circumstance, God will help you through these tough seasons.

> *God of all healing counsel! He comes alongside us when we go through hard times, and before you know it, he brings us alongside someone else who is going through hard times so that we can be there for that person just as God was there for us. We have plenty of hard times that come from following the Messiah, but no more so than the good times of his healing comfort—we get a full measure of that, too.* 2 Corinthians 1:4-5

Grieving is the best way THROUGH your pain.

Many people in our culture are not comfortable with grief. If they see you crying, they automatically want to build a dam for your tears and they will find ways to try to make you stop crying. Crying is a very healthy form of grieving. Let those tears flow with safe and healthy people in your life! If you try to have a brave face for these special days and a gulp it up mentality, it will only cause you greater pain in the end. Allowing yourself the time and space to grieve is important and it will ease the severity of the pain. This is a critical time to be in a support group to get the love you need.

"*Rain brings rainbows.*" – Jacke Van Woerkom

There are many ways that we can celebrate the anniversary of our child's life, their birthday, or the holidays. As moms we feel like we still need to take care of others and we don't always put ourselves first. Be released today to take care of yourself first. If you would like to do an activity in remembrance of your child in solitude, that is perfectly fine. Or if you'd like to take a few close friends with you to the grave site, don't feel compelled that you have to take the entire family. Do what is best and right for you to help you get into a better place for your own wellbeing.

> Some of these milestone dates may come up during the twelve weeks you are together. If a woman is struggling that week with a birthday or anniversary of their child's passing, give her some extra time in the group to share her feelings. These can be very tough days, and having the GM support group will help tremendously as the women go through their remembrance days.

Anniversaries, Birthdays & Holidays

Other Siblings

We can be so filled with grief at times that we forget about our other children and what they may be experiencing. Sometimes the ones that are the most silent are the ones to watch the most. As hard as it may be, reach out to your other children and involve them in these special occasions. Schedule a date just to spend with them!

Spindrift Thoughts

"I don't want my memory to fade of my beloved child."
Do something special that will create a remembrance for them.

> *The Master, Jesus...took bread. Having given thanks, he broke it and said, this is my body, broken for you. Do this to remember me. After supper, he did the same thing with the cup: this cup is my blood, my new covenant with you. Each time you drink this cup, remember me.*
> 1 Corinthians 11:24-25(MSG)

"I just want to be alone, but people won't let me."
It is okay to be alone, but just don't stay isolated.

> *As often as possible Jesus withdrew to out-of-the-way places for prayer.* Luke 5:16 (MSG)

"I don't want to decorate or even shop this year!"
Then don't! No one says you have to do any of it. You will do these activities when you are ready to do them again.

"I can't bear the thought of writing Christmas cards, but I know everyone wants to know how we are doing."

Don't fall into the guilt trap or people peacemaker mode. Take care of you. Your family and friends will understand.

> *Fearing people is a dangerous trap, but trusting the Lord means safety.* Proverbs 29:25 (NLT)

Quick Share

Share with the group any of these thoughts that have been reoccurring.

Anniversaries, Birthdays & Holidays

ANNIVERSARIES

The anniversary of your child's death signifies a huge milestone in our journey towards healing. The first anniversary of our child's death may be the hardest but there are ways to cope.

No one knows your child more than you, so allow your relationship with them to determine how you spend that day. Remember there isn't a text book way to climb this mountain. Allow God to be your trail guide and trust His direction that is specific for you.

GM COMMUNITY IDEAS

"Our first year we had a gathering at one of Tommy's favorite restaurants and then had a couple hours at the gravesite for people to come see our family. Now we go to a specific hamburger restaurant because that was Tommy's favorite!" – Didi

"My favorite thing to do is get a balloon, pour my heart out with a marker and write Jacqueline all over it, because I so rarely get to write her name on anything and it makes my heart so happy to write it. I release the balloon, pray and ask God to find her and give her a big hug and kiss from mommy and watch it go up to Heaven until I can't see it anymore." – Carrie

"The first year I went to the beach where we released my son's ashes. Then we went out to a nice dinner with the family and celebrated him." – Lisa

"The first anniversary of Randy's death was spent with our immediate family and we all went to Knott's Berry Farm sharing special times we've had with him. We chose to have fun and not be mourning his absence, because that's what he would've wanted us to do." – Jacke

BIRTHDAYS

Birthdays can be some of the most difficult times for us as a Grieving Moms. Our loving eyes were not intended to see the day they were born and the day they died. We carried them for nine months and celebrated each new year of development.

In addition, there are many special milestone birthdays in our society such as: first birthday, five-year birthday, sweet sixteen, or when they turn twenty-one years old.

Be aware siblings' birthdays are important, too. Many Grieving Moms do not realize that siblings may go through hard times when they come to milestone birthdays. They may go through a difficult time realizing that they are now the same age as when their sibling passed away, or the following

Anniversaries, Birthdays & Holidays

year when they are now one year older than the sibling who passed. It may be challenging to accept that they are now the 'older' child in the family. Having open communication with them is essential during this time.

Birthdays can be challenging times in the grieving process. It's simply not okay to experience this indescribable vacancy in our heart, especially when other moms are taking special requests from their children for their birthdays—like baking a cake.

Cry to release the pain, laugh at those funny memories and it's okay to experience anger, it's the secondary emotion of hurt and fear.

Everyone responds differently, so allow yourself to feel and face these days insulated in God's loving arms.

> *He will wipe every tear from their eyes. There will be no more death or mourning or crying or pain, for the old order of things has passed away.* Revelation 21:4

GM COMMUNITY IDEAS

"My son's birthday was only about a month after he died and we were still in our frozen phase. Experiencing his birthday that soon was almost unbearable, but we held each other together tightly. Phone calls and sending cards are now replaced with intentional reflective memories that bring us a smile and at times even a laugh of precious moments spent with him." –Jacke

"My son loved Disneyland, so I went there to celebrate his special day. When he was alive I always bought him a special gift, so when I went back I had to buy him a gift even though he wasn't here anymore." – Lisa

"My son was in a sober living house and I baked cookies and sat around the counter and talked to the men that were in his same program. It made me feel close to him again." –Sharon

"I baked my five-year-old daughter a birthday cake and brought it to the grave site and sang her favorite song. We brought long stem carnations and my other children spontaneously laid them end to end around her little grave because you could still see the outline from when she had been buried. It was so incredibly sweet and moving." – Carrie

Quick Share

Share with the group ways that you have gotten through your child's birthday or the anniversary of the Landslide.

Anniversaries, Birthdays & Holidays

HOLIDAYS

Holidays usually means time spent with our family and loved ones, but it can be an especially difficult time of year. It seems like everyone else is having a great time with their family, and all you can think about is how hard it is to not have your child with you. The holiday somehow magnifies your loss even more. If it is your first holiday without them, the pain seems even greater and you may not know how to navigate these challenging times. Be careful not to stuff the grief down to suppress the pain.

For some moms, they just want to be alone during the holidays and remember their child in their own special way. This is perfectly fine. The holidays will come back around the following year.

Other moms will want to be surrounded by family and friends and do things all together with the family to remember their child. There is no one way to grieve. Each mom will grieve in their own way.

GM COMMUNITY IDEAS

"I recall the day I went into our Christmas decorations and opening the box that had the stockings in it; I completely lost it! So, we decided not to hang up the stockings that first year. I always remember Kay Warren's words, "When you can–you will." –Jacke

"The first Christmas after Nick passed away I decided we were not going to celebrate (no tree, no decorations, no gifts, no party), then I changed my mind after reconsidering how unfair that would be to my family...that's not what Nicholas would have wanted. We still displayed his stocking with the rest of the family's stockings. We watched family videos on the laptop as a way to "see" him and "hear" him (to fill the void he left). We had a candy dish filled with his favorite candy (smarties), and hung his favorite ornament (Batman) on the tree." –Sharon

"Every year Jonathan's stocking is still hung with the others. One thing I would like to start doing is sending the money I would have used to buy him gifts to put towards making a difference in the lives of others...whether it be through a charity or sending gifts to a family in need." –Lisa

Tips to carry you through the holidays

- Know that the anticipation of the holiday may be harder than actually having to go through the holiday
- Have an exit strategy in place if it gets too overwhelming
  (i.e. drive your own car to the event in case you want to leave early)
- Prepare in advance what you will say if you need to leave early

Anniversaries, Birthdays & Holidays

- Surround yourself with supportive people
- Don't do more than you want and tell people what you need
- Feel all the emotions of the season, but don't feel guilty if there is joy, too

CREATING NEW MEMORIES

It is important to begin creating new memories. The old memories will not be forgotten, but creating new memories is important to our growth and moving through our grieving process. New memories can be a healthy blend of the past as well as how you will be remembering your child in a future sense. What you do is important and should release hope and celebration, not leading you back to tears and thoughts of regret and hopelessness.

Suggestions for creating new holiday traditions

- Light a candle for your child at the holiday table
- Tell some fun stories about your child
- Create a physical remembrance place in your house for them
- Say a prayer aloud as everyone gathers for the meal
- Create some new traditions in memory of your child
- Create a memory box
- Remember to include other siblings into activities
- Remember: not everyone grieves the same
- Donate to your child's favorite charity

Remembering Special Moments

"My son was cremated and I took some of his ashes and put them into a small container and wrote out Psalm 23 and gave it to friends and family that were not able to come to the funeral." –Sharon

"My son was cremated and I had some of his ashes put into a special tattoo I had drawn on my arm in remembrance of him." –Jacke

"I put up special pictures on social media on my son's birthday so that others can remember him like I do." –Allyson

"For my son's memorial, we set sail on a boat into the water and the dolphins surrounded our boat along with this bird that did not leave my side. I knew that my son was with me and I felt him as we were sailing on the water." –Lisa

Anniversaries, Birthdays & Holidays

"I was with a few other military moms who lost their sons and we all got the same special tattoo together." —Didi

"We put a special bench as a memorial where my daughter passed away. I took my other daughter with us and we both sat on the bench and talked together in this special place." —Shelley

"I had a special duck that came to my pool every day after my son passed away. It was not the normal season for ducks to be in my area, but I knew it was God's way of encouraging me. One day my duck was not there, so I looked up to God and with a strong voice said, 'I want my duck back', and immediately the duck flew into my pool from nowhere." —Jani

"I like to visit his grave site and put different things on his grave. One day I came and put carrots on his grave, just because he didn't like carrots! It was my way of joking with him and feeling close to him." —Barb

Activity

Circle some of the ideas from this session that resonated with you.
Share with the group any of these ideas that you'd like to do this year.

Moving Forward

Do something in remembrance of your child. Bring it with you next week to share.

Closing Prayer

Preview of Next Week

What we have learned
Next week we will reflect on what we have learned being in the GM support group and how that has helped us through the grieving process.

> The women may bring any item that they had made or that had been given to them as a remembrance of their child. If you see a really good idea that you'd like the GM program to consider offering to our moms, please email us at *info@grievingmoms.com*.
>
> Call or email the women in your group to remind them to bring their remembrance items next week.

Moving Forward Journal

List some ways in which you have remembered your child. It can be physical objects or new traditions that you are doing.

1. _____

2. _____

3. _____

4. _____

5. _____

6. _____

7. _____

SPECIAL NOTE

Bring any of these items to the GM group next week to share them with the group as a remembrance of your child.

Prayer Requests

Name:_____

Situation: _____

_____

_____

_____

Name:_____

Situation: _____

_____

_____

_____

Name:_____

Situation: _____

_____

_____

_____

Name:_____

Situation: _____

_____

_____

_____

Name:_____

Situation: _____

_____

_____

_____

What We Have Learned

SESSION ELEVEN

*"I can do things you cannot, you can do things I cannot;
together we can do great things."*
Mother Teresa

OPENING PRAYER

KEY SCRIPTURE

And the God of all grace, who called you to His eternal glory in Christ, after you have suffered a little while, will Himself restore you and make you strong, firm, and steadfast. I Peter 5:10

SHARING

We will honor our child's memory as we share their lives with the other Grieving Moms in the group.

VIDEO

Coming soon.

DISCUSSION

We will reflect on what we have learned by being in this GM support group and how it has helped each of us through the grieving process.

You will be surprised at how far the women in your group have come. Most of them will be experiencing some freedom and a new peace that they didn't have when they started. They have found support in a safe environment with other moms who know exactly what they are going through. They are learning how to trust Him, and through that, they are feeling some relief from their pain and sorrow. Spend some time having the women share their remembrance items. This is a special time for the moms to specifically share with the group about their child. Next week, the last week of your *Grieving Moms* group, you will be celebrating hope and new friends.

What We Have Learned

DISCUSSION

Tonight marks our eleventh week together as Grieving Moms. By sharing this journey, we have discovered that we are not alone. We have been able to identify the various phases and emotions that we experience as moms who have lost a child.

What we have learned

We have learned how to overcome triggers in our lives as well as honoring our child's memory on special occasions. We have been given tools for dealing with well-meaning friends that do not know how to be there for us, as well as some of the family dynamics revolving around our loss.

Most importantly, we have learned to trust and rely on God, who loves us dearly and wants us to live in peace and joy instead of in the pain brought on by our anger, disappointment, fear, guilt, and shame because of our grief.

This week we are going to look back and see the progress we have made as we have moved toward freedom through sharing with one another and by utilizing the tools we have been given.

 **Quick Activity**

Using a scale of 0 to 5 (0 meaning "not at all" and 5 meaning "significant achievement") how would you rate yourself in each of the following?

1. I am realizing I am not alone. ____
2. I am trusting God, that He's got my situation. ____
3. I am dealing with the disappointments. ____
4. I am working through the Landslide phases and entering the next phase. ____
5. I accept the fact that I may not always understand why. ____
6. I am beginning to experience peace and joy in my life again. ____
7. I am able to honor my child's memory in a beautiful way. ____
8. I have forgiven myself for any mistakes I've made. ____
9. I have forgiven God for anything that I have placed on Him. ____
10. I have been able to let go of some of my child's physical belongings. ____
11. I have been able to recognize and deal with trigger events in my life. ____
12. I am beginning to understand my family's way of dealing with grief. ____
13. I am better equipped to deal with things that other people say to me. ____
14. I have a better idea how to cope with holidays and special occasions. ____

What We Have Learned

◎ Quick Share

- Share your responses with the group.
- Discuss areas you would still like to work on.

> At the end of the sharing you will want to encourage your women with how far they have come. You may even want to say a few words about each one of them individually. They have worked hard and experienced healing and growth. It is important to acknowledge what God has done. This will help them continue on their journey of hope and healing.

A Time of Remembrance

One of the biggest fears of a Grieving Mom is that their child will be forgotten. In this community, we want to make sure that never happens. Simple things like saying our child's name, writing their name, or hearing their voice, fade as time goes by–yet we want their memory to always be with us.

One way the Grieving Moms in the community have honored their child's memory is by taking some of their possessions and making a special item from it. We discussed, in previous sessions, some ideas for doing this, and in this session you will get the opportunity to share those items and remember your child with a group of moms who completely understand you.

◎ Activity

Show the moms what you have brought to the group to remember your child.
Share why this item is so special to you.

Planning A Celebration Together

Next week we will be having a celebration of hope and new friends. Plan a potluck for next week. You can meet at the same place, or choose a special location for your event.

◎ Moving Forward

Reflect on how this group has helped you in moving forward in your journey towards finding hope.

What are some things you'd still like to work on that you have learned in this group?

What We Have Learned

"The Grieving Moms support group has helped me by being with other moms to remind me that I am not alone in my grief. There is nothing more healing than to connect with moms to learn how they cope. The material is encouraging and helpful to remind me that grief is a process and that God is always with me even when it doesn't feel like it." —Didi

"Being in this Grieving Moms group has confirmed in my heart that I need to be around other Grieving Moms in some capacity, both to offer compassion and support, but also to receive it. Every morning I wake up is another brand-new day that I must figure out how to live without my youngest child. The love and support I get from other Grieving Moms is an integral part of my continuous healing and being able to give back keeps me moving forward and from letting the grief consume me." —Carrie

Closing Prayer

Preview of Next Week

Celebration of Hope and New Friends

Next week we will be celebrating how far we have come and the new friends that we have made to support us in our journey.

What We Have Learned

PLANNING A CELEBRATION

Date: _____

Time: _____

Where: _____

What we will bring to share: _____

NAME:	**BRINGING:**
_____	_____
_____	_____
_____	_____
_____	_____
_____	_____
_____	_____
_____	_____
_____	_____
_____	_____
_____	_____

Moving Forward Journal

Reflect on how this group has helped you in moving forward in your journey towards finding hope.
_____
_____
_____
_____
_____
_____
_____
_____
_____
_____
_____
_____
_____

What are some things you'd still like to work on that you have learned in this group?
_____
_____
_____
_____
_____
_____
_____
_____
_____
_____
_____
_____
_____
_____

Prayer Requests

Name:_____

Situation: _____

_____

_____

_____

Name:_____

Situation: _____

_____

_____

_____

Name:_____

Situation: _____

_____

_____

_____

Name:_____

Situation: _____

_____

_____

_____

Name:_____

Situation: _____

_____

_____

_____

Celebration of Hope and New Friends

SESSION TWELVE

"In this Landslide, I'm celebrating each breath I take!"
Jacke Van Woerkom

This week you will celebrate what God has done for the women in your group over the past twelve weeks. It is important to recognize and celebrate the victories in our lives. Each woman in your group will have experienced some degree of healing by working through this process together, and you want to acknowledge that it is only through Jesus that this is possible. Be sure to give God the glory as you share the stories of what you have gotten out of the group.

At the end of the group many of the women will be fearful because they do not want to quit seeing each other. If you are a local group, you can go for walks or other activities together. Whether you are in a local group or an online group, we highly encourage you to start a private Facebook page. Please name it *Grieving Moms* (then add whatever name to this you'd like). We will provide you with the official *Grieving Moms* logo to put on the banner of your FB page. For example, *Grieving Moms* – Orange County CA.

In the near future, we will put together some GM Care and Support Groups so that the women can continue to get the support they need.

OPENING PRAYER

KEY SCRIPTURE
They celebrate Your abundant goodness and joyfully sing of Your righteousness. Psalm 145:7

SHARING
Share how this GM support group has helped you in your journey through grief.

VIDEO
Coming soon.

DISCUSSION
Celebrating friendship and finding hope with the moms in our group.

Celebration of Hope and New Friends

DISCUSSION

In this group time we celebrate, not necessarily because we are no longer grieving, but because we are learning how to have hope and even joy in the midst of our pain.

We have developed close, loving, and trusting relationships through this GM support group. Encourage each other, continue to pray for one another, and hold each other accountable in using the tools we have learned.

God has definitely shown up in our group. God's goodness is abundant and we have learned to seek comfort and wisdom from the Scriptures and with each other.

He has been with us week after week as we have looked to Him for our healing and hope. We can take comfort in knowing that His promises are real and we can confidently put our trust in Him.

Activity

Look at **"What's Next"** and circle two things you would like to do next.

What's Next?

Options
Circle two things you'd like to do next.

1. Read one of the resource books that are suggested on the following page or at www.GrievingMoms.com

2. Which ones? _____

3. Repeat Grieving Moms, Finding Hope—Resurfacing support group

4. Sign up for the next level of the Grieving Moms, Finding Hope group

5. Join a study group at your local church

6. Join another grief group in your area

→ Share with the group what you have committed to do next in your healing process.

Celebration of Hope and New Friends

> Sharing aloud is a great means of accountability. The women in your group will be more likely to follow through with taking next steps if they have told the rest of the group what they plan to do.
>
> We suggest that following the last meeting you send an email or text to the women in your group encouraging them to continue their journey to healing and wholeness.

 Moving Forward

Think about ways you are recognizing God working in your life since joining the group. Journal your thoughts.

SPECIAL NOTE

If your group has not already done so consider doing the following:

- Start a <u>private</u> Facebook group with the name Grieving Moms in the title.
- Start a group text message
- Write down everyone's contact info at the back of this guide book.

 Closing Prayer

> **A Note to the Leader:**
>
> Now that you have completed a twelve-week *Grieving Moms, Finding Hope* group we encourage you to identify one or more potential new leaders for upcoming groups. You can be a huge encouragement and support to future new leaders because you have already experienced the unique privilege of being a GM leader, and you have abundant wisdom to offer them.
>
> Don't forget to encourage your group to continue on the journey to healing by going through this group again, joining a GM Care and Support group, and by staying in contact with each other.
>
> We pray that you have been richly blessed as you have led this group. Thank you for your leadership!

Resources

Website
www.GrievingMoms.com

Email
info@GrievingMoms.com

Sign up for your daily encouraging words "Hope at Sunrise."

Jacke Van Woerkom has put together words of encouragement using some of the Scriptures that have inspired her along her journey as a Grieving Mom. She hopes that they will bring you comfort and peace as you go through each day.
Sign up at **www.GrievingMoms.com**

⇢ SISTER SUPPORT GROUP
- Hurting Moms, Mending Hearts www.hurtingmoms.com

⇢ RECOMMENDED READING
- A Journey Out of the Wilderness (book) by Sherry Lynn Ward
- A Journey Out of the Wilderness (blog) www.sherrylynnward.com
- The Story of a Hurting Mom (book) by Cathy Taylor
- A Grace Disguised (book) by Jerry Sittser
- Streams in the Desert (online devotional) – L.B. Cowman
- You'll Get Through This (book) by Max Lucado

⇢ RECOMMENDED WEBSITES
- www.GrievingMoms.com – For Hope in the Landslide
- www.HurtingMoms.com – For moms who are experiencing hurt over the choices and actions of their teen or adult children
- www.BlueLetterBible.org – For Bible verses and original language

⇢ COUNSELING
- SOZO – www.bethel.com/ministries/bethel-sozo-international

Moving Forward Journal

Think about ways you are recognizing God working in your life since joining the group. Journal your thoughts.

Prayer Requests

Name:_____

Situation: _____

_____

_____

_____

Name:_____

Situation: _____

_____

_____

_____

Name:_____

Situation: _____

_____

_____

_____

Name:_____

Situation: _____

_____

_____

_____

Name:_____

Situation: _____

_____

_____

_____

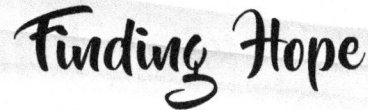

> These are tips for the women, which will help them to continue to grow in their relationship with Jesus and to experience further healing in their lives.

PRAY

It can be helpful to write out our prayers as if we are writing a letter to God. This prevents our minds from wandering as we pray and helps us to stay focused on the things that we want to talk to Him about. It also may be helpful for you to pray aloud. You could pray in the car as you are driving, or in the shower or while on a walk, whatever works for you. Let your feelings flow as you pray, remembering that prayer is simply talking to God. It doesn't have to be fancy–just speak or write from your heart.

WORSHIP

Worship can be expressed in many ways such as: singing, dancing, or spending time in nature meditating on the goodness of God. Worshipping softens our hearts and opens us up to experiencing God's presence. When we worship we need to put everything else aside and simply focus on praising God. Even in the midst of sadness and pain we can find things to be grateful for, and it is important to think about those things and to express our thanks to Him. Find a place where you can be free to worship uninhibitedly, whether it is in your bedroom, in your car, at the beach or park.

READ SCRIPTURE

The Bible is our handbook for life and it is full of promises from God. Reading the Bible will comfort and sustain us and it will give us direction for handling and responding to every situation. When we open our Bible we allow the words of Scripture to penetrate our hearts. This draws us closer to God and we begin to experience peace, joy, and hope. When you discover a verse or a passage that speaks to you, read it over and over again, memorize it, journal about it. When it comes to reading the Bible, don't just skim over it, take time to dig in deep. As time goes on, the more you read the Bible, the better you will understand God and how great His love is towards you and your child.

JOURNAL

Journaling is a great way to express our feelings. It helps us to organize and unload our thoughts. When our head is filled with so many cares, especially negative or painful thoughts, we can find release and relief by writing them down. Journaling our prayers and important verses or passages of Scripture enable us to see what God is doing in our lives.

EMAIL SIGN-UP

Sign up for the daily encouraging words "**Hope at Sunrise**" at www.grievingmoms.com.

Grieving Moms, Finding Hope Group List

NAME_____ PHONE_____
EMAIL_____

NAME_____ PHONE_____
EMAIL_____

NAME_____ PHONE_____
EMAIL_____

NAME_____ PHONE_____
EMAIL_____

NAME_____ PHONE_____
EMAIL_____

NAME_____ PHONE_____
EMAIL_____

NAME_____ PHONE_____
EMAIL_____

NAME_____ PHONE_____
EMAIL_____

NAME_____ PHONE_____
EMAIL_____

NAME_____ PHONE_____
EMAIL_____

NAME_____ PHONE_____
EMAIL_____

Scriptures for Encouragement

Welcome Letter

We are hard pressed on every side, but not crushed; perplexed, but not in despair; persecuted, but not abandoned; struck down, but not destroyed. We always carry around in our body the death of Jesus, so that the life of Jesus may also be revealed in our body. – 2 Corinthians 4:8-10

Being confident of this, He who began a good work in you will carry it on to completion until the day of Christ Jesus. – Philippians 1:6

Though the mountains be shaken and the hills be removed, yet my unfailing love for you will not be shaken nor my covenant of peace be removed, says the Lord, who has compassion on you.
– Isaiah 54:10

Session One

We are hard pressed on every side, but not crushed; perplexed, but not in despair; persecuted, but not abandoned; struck down, but not destroyed. We always carry around in our body the death of Jesus, so that the life of Jesus may also be revealed in our body. – 2 Corinthians 4:8-10

And now, here's what I'm going to do: I'm going to start all over again. I'm taking her back out into the wilderness where we had our first date, and I'll court her. I'll give her bouquets of roses. I'll turn Heartbreak Valley into Acres of Hope. – Hosea 2:14-15a (MSG)

The LORD is near to the brokenhearted and saves the crushed in spirit. – Psalm 34:18 (ESV)

He heals the brokenhearted and binds up their wounds. – Psalm 147:3 (ESV)

For this child I prayed, and the Lord has granted me my petition that I made to him. Therefore I have lent him to the Lord. As long as he lives, he is lent to the Lord." And he worshiped the Lord there.
– 1 Samuel 1:27-28 (ESV)

Blessed are those who mourn, for they shall be comforted. – Matthew 5:4 (ESV)

And regarding the question, friends, that has come up about what happens to those already dead and buried, we don't want you in the dark any longer. First off, you must not carry on over them like people who have nothing to look forward to, as if the grave were the last word. Since Jesus died and broke loose from the grave, God will most certainly bring back to life those who died in Jesus. And then this: We can tell you with complete confidence—we have the Master's word on it—that when the Master comes again to get us, those of us who are still alive will not get a jump on the dead and leave them behind. In actual fact, they'll be ahead of us. The Master himself will give the command. Archangel thunder! God's

Scriptures for Encouragement

trumpet blast! He'll come down from heaven and the dead in Christ will rise—they'll go first. Then the rest of us who are still alive at the time will be caught up with them into the clouds to meet the Master. Oh, we'll be walking on air! And then there will be one huge family reunion with the Master. So reassure one another with these words. – I Thessalonians 4:13-17 (MSG)

Who comforts us in all our affliction, so that we may be able to comfort those who are in any affliction, with the comfort with which we ourselves are comforted by God. – 2 Corinthians 1:4 (ESV)

It is the L{\sc ord} who goes before you. He will be with you; he will not leave you or forsake you. Do not fear or be dismayed. – Deuteronomy 31:8 (ESV)

When they arrive at the gates of death, G{\sc od} welcomes those who love him. Oh, G{\sc od}, here I am, your servant, your faithful servant: set me free for your service! I'm ready to offer the thanksgiving sacrifice and pray in the name of G{\sc od}. – Psalm 116:14-17 (MSG)

Behold, the dwelling place of God is with man. He will dwell with them, and they will be his people, and God himself will be with them as their God. He will wipe away every tear from their eyes, and death shall be no more, neither shall there be mourning, nor crying, nor pain anymore, for the former things have passed away. And he who was seated on the throne said, Behold, I am making all things new. Also he said, Write this down, for these words are trustworthy and true. – Revelation 21:3b-5 (ESV)

Your eyes saw my unformed substance; in your book were written, every one of them, the days that were formed for me, when as yet there was none of them. – Psalm 139:16 (ESV)

For I know the plans I have for you, declares the L{\sc ord}, plans for welfare and not for evil, to give you a future and a hope. – Jeremiah 29:11 (ESV)

To the choirmaster: according to The Doe of the Dawn. A Psalm of David. My God, my God, why have you forsaken me? Why are you so far from saving me, from the words of my groaning? O my God, I cry by day, but you do not answer, and by night, but I find no rest. Yet you are holy, enthroned on the praises of Israel. In you our fathers trusted; they trusted, and you delivered them. To you they cried and were rescued; in you they trusted and were not put to shame. – Psalm 22:1-8 (ESV)

He will wipe away every tear from their eyes, and death shall be no more, neither shall there be mourning, nor crying, nor pain anymore, for the former things have passed away. – Revelation 21:4 (ESV)

Since therefore the children share in flesh and blood, he himself likewise partook of the same things, that through death he might destroy the one who has the power of death, that is, the devil.
– Hebrews 2:14 (ESV)

Scriptures for Encouragement

Session Two

We are pressed on every side by troubles, but we are not crushed. We are perplexed, but not driven to despair...we get knocked down, but we are not destroyed. – 2 Corinthians 4:8-9 (NLT)

The Lord himself goes before you and will be with you; he will never leave you nor forsake you. Do not be afraid; do not be discouraged. – Deuteronomy 31:8

The accuser of our brothers and sisters, who accuses them before our God day and night, has been hurled down. – Revelation 12:10b

No weapon that is fashioned against you shall succeed, and you shall refute every tongue that rises against you in judgment. This is the heritage of the servants of the Lord and their vindication from me, declares the Lord. – Isaiah 54:17 (ESV)

Why, my soul, are you downcast? Why so disturbed within me? Put your hope in God, for I will yet praise him, my Savior and my God. – Psalm 42:5

Therefore judge nothing before the appointed time; wait till the Lord comes. He will bring to light what is hidden in darkness and will expose the motives of men's hearts. At that time each will receive his praise from God. – 1 Corinthians 4:5

Session Three

See, I am doing a new thing! Now it springs up; do you not perceive it? – Isaiah 43:19a

Are you tired? Worn out? Burned out on religion? Come to me. Get away with me and you'll recover your life. I'll show you how to take a real rest. Walk with me and work with me—watch how I do it. Learn the unforced rhythms of grace. I won't lay anything heavy or ill-fitting on you. Keep company with me and you'll learn to live freely and lightly. – Matthew 11:28-30 (MSG)

I'm not saying that I have this all together, that I have it made. But I am well on my way, reaching out for Christ, who has so wondrously reached out for me. – Philippians 3:12 (MSG)

Then I heard a strong voice out of Heaven saying, Salvation and power are established! Kingdom of our God, authority of his Messiah! The Accuser of our brothers and sisters thrown out, who accused them day and night before God. They defeated him through the blood of the Lamb and the bold word of their witness. – Revelation 12:10 (MSG)

For God did not send his Son into the world to condemn the world, but in order that the world might be saved through him. – John 3:17 (ESV)

Scriptures for Encouragement

God met me more than halfway, he freed me from my anxious fears. Look at him; give him your warmest smile. Never hide your feelings from him. – Psalm 34:4-5 (MSG)

My beloved friends, let us continue to love each other since love comes from God. Everyone who loves is born of God and experiences a relationship with God. The person who refuses to love doesn't know the first thing about God, because God is love—so you can't know him if you don't love. – I John 4:7-8 (MSG)

But they will have to give account to him who is ready to judge the living and the dead.
– 1 Peter 4:5

Session Four

I'm not saying that I have this all together, that I have it made. But I am well on my way, reaching out for Christ, who has so wondrously reached out for me...I've got my eye on the goal, where God is beckoning us onward—to Jesus...and I'm not turning back. – Philippians 3:12-14 (MSG)

I'll be with you as you do this, day after day after day, right up to the end of the age.
– Matthew 28:20b (MSG)

If you don't know what you're doing, pray to the Father. He loves to help. You'll get his help, and won't be condescended to when you ask for it. Ask boldly, believingly, without a second thought.
– James 1:5-6a (MSG)

God's Spirit is right alongside helping us along. If we don't know how or what to pray, it doesn't matter. He does our praying in and for us, making prayer out of our wordless sighs, our aching groans. He knows us far better than we know ourselves...and keeps us present before God. That's why we can be so sure that every detail in our lives of love for God is worked into something good. – Romans 8:26b-28

No doubt about it! God is good—good to good people, good to the good-hearted. But I nearly missed it, missed seeing his goodness. I was looking the other way...What's going on here? Is God out to lunch? Nobody's tending the store. The wicked get by with everything; they have it made, piling up riches; I've been stupid to play by the rules; what has it gotten me? A long run of bad luck, that's what—a slap in the face every time I walk out the door. If I'd have given in and talked like this, I would have betrayed your dear children...(Then) I entered the sanctuary of God. Then I saw the whole picture...I'm still in your presence, but you've taken my hand. You wisely and tenderly lead me, and then you bless me. You're all I want in heaven! You're all I want on earth! When my skin sags and my bones get brittle, God is rock-firm and faithful...I'm in the very presence of God—oh, how refreshing it is! I've made Lord God my home. God, I'm telling the world what you do! – Psalm 73:1-4, 11-16, 20-28 (MSG)

Scriptures for Encouragement

God is a safe place to hide, ready to help when we need him. We stand fearless at the cliff-edge of doom, courageous in sea storm and earthquake, Before the rush and roar of oceans, the tremors that shift mountains. Jacob-wrestling God fights for us, GOD-of-Angel-Armies protects us. – Psalm 46:1-3 (MSG)

When I said, 'My foot is slipping,' your unfailing love, Lord, supported me. When anxiety was great within me, your consolation brought me joy. – Psalm 94-18-19

I'll show up and take care of you as I promised and bring you back home. I know what I'm doing. I have it all planned out—plans to take care of you, not abandon you, plans to give you the future you hope for. – Jeremiah 29:10b-11 (MSG)

This is what the Lord says: 'When people fall down, do they not get up? When someone turns away, do they not return?' – Jeremiah 8:4

Whatever I have, wherever I am, I can make it through anything in the One who makes me who I am. – Philippians 4:13 (MSG)

Session Five

Do not be anxious about anything, but in everything by prayer and supplication with thanksgiving let your requests be made known to God. And the peace of God, which surpasses all understanding, will guard your hearts and your minds in Christ Jesus. – Philippians 4:6-7 (ESV)

We demolish arguments and every pretension that sets itself up against the knowledge of God, and we take captive every thought to make it obedient to Christ. – 2 Corinthians 10:5

And I will ask the Father, and he will give you another Advocate, who will never leave you. He is the Holy Spirit, who leads into all truth. The world cannot receive him, because it isn't looking for him and doesn't recognize him. But you know him, because he lives with you now and later will be in you.
– John 14:16-17 (NLT)

Don't drink too much wine. That cheapens your life. Drink the Spirit of God, huge draughts of him. Sing hymns instead of drinking songs! Sing songs from your heart to Christ. Sing praises over everything, any excuse for a song to God the Father in the name of our Master, Jesus Christ.
– Ephesians 5:18-20 (MSG)

Peace I leave with you; my peace I give to you. Not as the world gives do I give to you. Let not your hearts be troubled, neither let them be afraid. – John 14:27a (ESV)

Scriptures for Encouragement

Do not join those who drink too much wine or gorge themselves on meat, for drunkards and gluttons become poor, and drowsiness clothes them in rags. – Proverbs 23:20-21 (NIV)

The world is unprincipled. It's dog-eat-dog out there! The world doesn't fight fair. But we don't live or fight our battles that way—never have and never will. – 2 Corinthians 10:3 (MSG)

Session Six

Families love through all kinds of weather, and families stick together in all kinds of trouble.
– Proverbs 17:17 (MSG)

Session Seven

Bear with each other and forgive one another if any of you has a grievance against someone. Forgive as the Lord forgave you. – Colossians 3:13

We know that in all things God works for the good of those who love him, who have been called according to his purpose. – Romans 8:28

The LORD is good to all; he has compassion on all he has made – Psalm 145:9

We don't always know the why, but we do know that God will work it into good in the end.
He knows us far better than we know ourselves, knows our pregnant condition, and keeps us present before God. That's why we can be so sure that every detail in our lives of love for God is worked into something good. – Romans 8:27-28 (MSG)

Be gentle with one another, sensitive. Forgive one another as quickly and thoroughly as God in Christ forgave you. – Ephesians 4:32b (MSG)

You are good and do only good; make me follow your lead. – Psalm 119:68 (TLB)

For I know the plans I have for you…plans for welfare and not for evil, to give you a future and a hope.
– Jeremiah 29:11 (ESV)

You…were called to be free. But do not use your freedom to indulge the flesh. - Galatians 5:13a
He knows us far better than we know ourselves…That's why we can be so sure that every detail in our lives…is worked into something good. – Romans 8:28 (MSG)

For godly grief produces a repentance that leads to salvation without regret. – 2 Corinthians 7:10a (ESV)

Scriptures for Encouragement

Session Eight

I prayed for this child, and the Lord has granted me what I asked of him. So now I give him to the Lord. For his whole life he will be given over to the Lord. – I Samuel 1:27-28a

Jesus said to her, "I am the resurrection and the life. Whoever believes in me, though he die, yet shall he live, and everyone who lives and believes in me shall never die. Do you believe this?"
– John 11:25-26 (ESV)

Fear not, for I am with you; be not dismayed, for I am your God; I will strengthen you, I will help you, I will uphold you with my righteous right hand. – Isaiah 41:10 (ESV)

He will wipe away every tear from their eyes, and death shall be no more, neither shall there be mourning, nor crying, nor pain anymore, for the former things have passed away." – Revelation 21:4 (ESV)

This is how much God loved the world: He gave his Son, his one and only Son. And this is why: so that no one need be destroyed; by believing in him, anyone can have a whole and lasting life. God didn't go to all the trouble of sending his Son merely to point an accusing finger, telling the world how bad it was. He came to help, to put the world right again. – John 3:16-17 (MSG)

Session Nine

Be kind to one another, tenderhearted, forgiving one another, as God in Christ forgave you.
– Ephesians 4:32 (ESV)

A gentle answer turns away wrath, but a harsh word stirs up anger. – Proverbs 15:1

Now that we know what we have—Jesus, this great High Priest with ready access to God—let's not let it slip through our fingers. We don't have a priest who is out of touch with our reality. He's been through weakness and testing, experienced it all—all but the sin. So let's walk right up to him and get what he is so ready to give. Take the mercy, accept the help. – Hebrews 4:14-16

Bearing with one another and, if one has a complaint against another, forgiving each other; as the Lord has forgiven you, so you also must forgive. – Colossians 3:13 (ESV)

Do not repay evil for evil or reviling for reviling, but on the contrary, bless, for to this you were called, that you may obtain a blessing. – I Peter 3:9 (ESV)

Jesus said, "Father, forgive them, for they do not know what they are doing." And they divided up his clothes by casting lots. – Luke 23-34

Scriptures for Encouragement

Session Ten

When he had given thanks, he broke it and said…do this in remembrance of me. – 1 Corinthians 11:24

The Master, Jesus…took bread. Having given thanks, he broke it and said, this is my body, broken for you. Do this to remember me. After supper, he did the same thing with the cup: this cup is my blood, my new covenant with you. Each time you drink this cup, remember me. What you must solemnly realize is that every time you eat this bread and every time you drink this cup, you reenact in your words and actions the death of the Master. You will be drawn back to this meal again and again until the Master returns. You must never let familiarity breed contempt. – 1 Corinthians 11:24-26 (MSG)

As often as possible Jesus withdrew to out-of-the-way places for prayer. – Luke 5:16 (MSG)

Fearing people is a dangerous trap, but trusting the Lord means safety. – Proverbs 29:25 (NLT)

Session Eleven

And the God of all grace, who called you to His eternal glory in Christ, after you have suffered a little while, will Himself restore you and make you strong, firm, and steadfast. – I Peter 5:10

Session Twelve

They celebrate Your abundant goodness and joyfully sing of Your righteousness. – Psalm 145:7

Guest Speaker Opportunity

INVITE JACKE VAN WOERKOM TO SPEAK

Certified Life Coach Jacke Van Woerkom is no stranger to personal trials, on January 15th, she faced the loss of her son due to suicide. Through her faith and the strength she found in her support community, Jacke gained a contagious spirit of hope, which she brings to others through speaking, coaching and workshops.

Determined to see others succeed and find balance and purpose in the midst of life's darkest moments, Jacke serves as a lay counselor at Saddleback Community Church in Southern California. Her passionate heart reaches out towards other Grieving Moms who have suffered the loss of a child, creating opportunities for healing and helping them find hope through God.

Invite Jacke to speak to your group about a host of topics related to being a grieving mom.

Topics

- ➔ **Hope for Grieving Moms**
- ➔ **Developing Your Mission Statement**
- ➔ **The Tiger & The Little Girl —Don't Hide Behind Your Bold Stripes**
- ➔ **Adventure – Get Up and Out of Your Slippers**
- ➔ **God's Backpack – Satisfied with your Gifts and Offload the Heavy Stuff**

Book Jacke to speak   info@squaretreepublishing.com
Purchase Resources   www.grievingmoms.com

Guest Speaker Opportunity

INVITE SHERRY LYNN WARD TO SPEAK

CEO of Square Tree Publishing and Director of **Hurting Moms, Mending Hearts**, Sherry Ward is passionate about bringing hope to those who need it most. After years of battling a debilitating disease that plagued both her and her family, she authored *A Journey Out of the Wilderness*, her story of making sense out of life's struggles. A Southern California college professor who holds an M.A. in Counseling, Sherry uses her eclectic background in education, business, and counseling to equip others on their journey to find hope, healing, and restoration.

ENCOURAGEMENT TO MAKE IT THROUGH A WILDERNESS SEASON OF LIFE

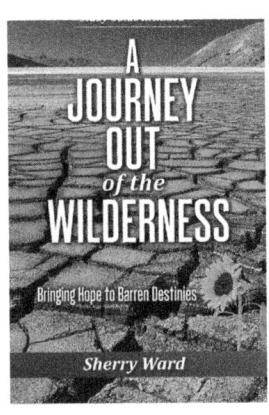

Going through a Wilderness experience and feel like giving up? Get a fresh perspective from where you are –*A Journey Out of the Wilderness* will take you from, "Will this ever end?" to "This was the most transformational time of my life!"

Filled with insights and revelations God gave her in the Wilderness, Sherry Lynn Ward's book reveals her heart towards the hurting, those needing courage to keep on going. *A Journey Out of the Wilderness* offers hope that you will come out of your Wilderness, be launched into your destiny and into your own personal Promised Land!

Topics

- → Receiving your breakthrough
- → Hope through the Wilderness Season
- → Breaking off lies you are believing
- → How to write your first book
- → Stop chasing the shiny object – Finding your big 'Yes'

Book Sherry to speak	info@squaretreepublishing.com
Blogs	www.sherrylynnward.com
Purchase Book	www.grievingmoms.com/shop or Amazon

At **SQUARE TREE PUBLISHING**, we believe your message matters. That is why our dedicated team of professionals is committed to bringing your literary texts and targeted curriculum to a global marketplace. We strive to make that message of the highest quality, while still maintaining your voice. We believe in you, therefore, we provide a platform through website design, blogs, and social media campaigns to showcase your unique message. Our innovative team offers a full range of services: from editing to graphic design, inspired with an eye for excellence so your message is clearly and distinctly heard.

Whether you are a new writer needing guidance with each step of the process, or a seasoned writer, we will propel you to the next level of your development.

At **SQUARE TREE PUBLISHING,** it's all about **you.**

Take advantage of a free consultation.
Your opportunity is "Write Outside the Box"!

www.SquareTreePublishing.com

www.GrievingMoms.com

Made in the USA
Columbia, SC
29 March 2023